mPalermu, Dancers, and Other Plays

◆

mPalermu, Dancers, and Other Plays

EMMA DANTE

Translated from the Sicilian, Neapolitan,
and Italian, and with an Introduction by
Francesca Spedalieri

SWAN
ISLE
PRESS

Emma Dante is one of the most exciting Italian theatre makers of the 21st century. A playwright, deviser, and director, she graduated in 1990 from the Accademia Nazionale d'Arte Drammatica Silvio D'Amico in Rome. Since 1999, she has been the artistic director of the Palermo-based award-winning theatre company Compagnia Sud Costa Occidentale.

Francesca Spedalieri is visiting assistant professor of English and Women's, Gender, and Sexuality Studies at Stony Brook University— The State University of New York.

Swan Isle Press, Chicago 60628
© 2020 by Swan Isle Press
All rights reserved. Published 2020.
Printed in the United States of America
First Edition
24 23 22 21 20   1 2 3 4 5
ISBN-13: 978-0-9972287-5-5 (paperback)

Originally published as:
Carnezzeria: trilogia della famiglia siciliana
    Includes: *mPalermu*, *Carnezzeria*, and *Vita mia*
    2007 Fazi Editore, Rome.
    © Mondadori Libri S.p.A. / Rizzoli, Milan
Cani di bancata
    2007 Hystrio, Abano Terme. Padua
    © Mondadori Libri S.p.A. / Rizzoli, Milan
Trilogia degli occhiali
    © 2011 RCS Libri S.p.A., Milan
    © 2018 Mondadori Libri S.p.A. / Rizzoli, Milan

Library of Congress Cataloging-in-Publication Data
Names: Dante, Emma, 1967- author. | Spedalieri, Francesca, translator, writer of introduction.
Title: mPalermu, dancers, and other plays / Emma Dante ; translated from the Sicilian, Neapolitan, Italian, and with an introduction by Francesca Spedalieri.
Description: First edition. | Chicago : Swan Isle Press, [2020] | Includes bibliographical references and index
Identifiers: LCCN 2019034232 | ISBN 9780997228755 (paperback ; alk paper)
Subjects: LCSH: Dante, Emma, 1967--- Translations into English.
Classification: LCC PQ4904.A58 A2 2019 | DDC 852/.92--dc23
LC record available at https://lccn.loc.gov/2019034232

Swan Isle Press gratefully acknowledges that this book was made possible, in part, with the generous support of the following:

STONY BROOK UNIVERSITY —
The State University of New York

THE GOLDEN MERCER CHARITABLE GIVING FUND

EUROPE BAY GIVING TRUST

AND OTHER KIND DONORS

The paper used in this publication meets the minimum requirements of the American National Standard for Information Sciences— Permanence of Paper for Printed Library Materials

ad Adriana, mia madre
a Dario, mio fratello
ho visto le stelle cadere

‑‑

to Adriana, my mother
to Dario, my brother
I saw the stars fall

— EMMA DANTE

CONTENTS

ILLUSTRATIONS

The photographs of Palermo and Sicily that
introduce each of the plays are
courtesy of the photographer, Carmine Maringola.

ACKNOWLEDGMENTS

This publication was made possible by a generous Research Initiative Grant for Faculty in the Fine Arts, Humanities, and Lettered Social Sciences (FAHSS) supported by the Offices of the Provost, Vice President for Research, and the Dean of the College of Arts and Sciences at Stony Brook University. I also wish to express my sincere gratitude to Ana Elena Puga and Charles Klopp, for their guidance in translating these plays. A heartfelt thank you goes to Lesley Ferris, Jennifer Schlueter, The Ohio State University Department of Theatre, the J. Lawrence and R. E. Lee Theatre Research Institute, the Coca-Cola Critical Difference for Women Grant Committee, The Ohio State University Alumni Grants for Graduate Research and Scholarship Committee and Frank Mauceri for believing in my passion for contemporary Italian theatre. These translations would have not been written without their encouragement and contributions to my fieldwork in Italy. I am indebted to the friends and colleagues of Compagnia Sud Costa Occidentale for their willingness to share their wealth of knowledge and invaluable archival material and to the countless artists – including Pamela Decker, Max Glenn, Shelby Brewster, Sifiso Mazibuko, Sarah Ware, Riley Hutchison, and Alex Kyle-Dipietropaolo – and wonderful individuals and organizations who have taken part in, supported, and funded staged readings and productions of these plays. Lastly, my biggest thank yous go to my dad, for diving back with me into our Sicilian language, to my friend Elizabeth Wellman, for bearing to listen to dozens of iterations of the same sentence, to my partner, Il Memming Park, for his invaluable input, and to Emma Dante, who has been and will continue to be an inspiration for my own work.

INTRODUCTION
Translating Dante's *Scrittura Scenica*

When I first stumbled on the works of Emma Dante, I was in search of a unicorn. As a theatre artist and scholar, I had primarily encountered Italian theatre through an English lens despite having been born in Sicily and having grown up in a small village in Basilicata. The sparks of nationalist pride I felt at every mention of Italy throughout my undergraduate and graduate school courses in the United States gradually led me to an unsettling realization: the larger narrative surrounding Italian theatre was constructed as a series of disconnected, mostly male, genius-driven spurts of activity occurring before the turn of the twenty-first century. These instances foregrounded the important contributions of commedia dell'arte, the Italian Futurists, Luigi Pirandello, Dario Fo, Romeo Castellucci's company Societàs Raffaello Sanzio and, in rare cases, the actor Eleonora Duse. I was discouraged by the lack of documentation of the contributions of southern Italian artists and, in particular, of women directors, devisers, and playwrights. Yet, I challenged what seemed to me to be a reductive approach to history given the complexity of the cultural forces on the Italian peninsula and my various encounters with them. So I started searching - first digitally, then physically. I combed through theatre and university archives, yearning to dig out what I knew had been omitted from the international theatrical discourse. And then, almost by accident, I found Emma Dante and her theatre company Compagnia Sud Costa Occidentale. I was captivated. The plays conceived and staged by Dante and devised with her company told tales of resistance and revolt against the social, political, and economic conditions of a familiar Sicily and southern Italy. They spoke of disenfranchisement, of gender inequality and oppression, of economic disparity between the North and South of the country, of deep-set bigotry, and of religious hypocrisy. Moreover, they resonated with my own directorial aesthetic predilection for visceral, physical storytelling.

Dante's stories undertake an irreverent subversion of the *status quo* akin to that of Dario Fo and Franca Rame's plays. At the same time, they encapsulate beautiful, often unsettling imagery and call for extreme physicality, much like the works of Romeo Castellucci. Further, in a similar fashion to the theatre of Eduardo De Filippo or Pirandello, they successfully incorporate cultural and linguistic elements native to Sicily and the South without ever becoming folkloric. Exemplifying a woman-lead "civic theatre" that provides a point of entrance into the everyday life of Southern Italy, Dante's artistic presence ultimately confirmed my suspicions surrounding the exclusion of women and southern Italian theatre from the contemporary national and international discourse, ripping through the narrative that my English-based knowledge of Italian theatre had constructed.

As Dante has often repeated in her interviews, she realized early in life that being a southern Italian woman – a Palermitan woman – meant that she could not afford to grow up with the luxury of innocence. Although raised in a middle class family, like many other Palermitans she negotiated a reality dominated by corruption, organized crime, poverty, and indolence. Together with the members of her company, she chose to capture snapshots of those who live at the margins of society while residing at the fringes of Italy. For her, to know, to understand, and to embody these southern Italian stories on stage became a necessity. Her plays thus stem from a need to confront herself and her audience with important questions regarding contemporary Sicily, and largely, the whole Italian peninsula. Dante regards the theatre as a site for listening to those who are not given a voice anywhere else; for witnessing abject bodies and their stories while staring them in the eyes; for engaging performers and audiences alike in a dialogue for change.

The seven plays anthologized in this collection were devised by Dante and her company during the seventeen years of the Berlusconi Era (1994-2011). Reminiscent of Beckett and Chekov in their focus on physicality, cyclicality, and dark humor, the plays oscillate between the ridiculous and the tragic of everyday life. The first three plays, *mPalermu* (2001), *The Butchery* (*Carnezzeria*, 2002), and *Life of Mine* (*Vita mia*, 2004), form *The Trilogy of the Sicilian Family*. *mPalermu* is a musing on the city of Palermo: an embodiment of the city's immobility and waste. The play portrays the Carollo family's fruitless attempt to leave their house for a Sunday stroll.

Lined up at the threshold, the five relatives are forever caught in a permanent act of going as they inevitably fail to accomplish their goal. *The Butchery* tells the story of Nina and her three brothers as the family prepares for a wedding that will never take place. Old family photographs reveal the violence to which the brothers have subjected their pregnant sister and the horrors the Cuore siblings lived while growing up in their small Sicilian town. Lastly, *Life of Mine* is a funeral wake for the youngest of the Calafiore brothers. It captures the instant in which the young man's soul detaches itself from his body and his mother's desperate attempt to keep it – and thus him – from leaving her forever.

The fourth play of this anthology, *Market Dogs* (*Cani di bancata*, 2006) is an allegorical representation of *Cosa Nostra* (the Sicilian mafia), its inner workings, and its interactions with individuals unaffiliated with the organization. The play paints mafia realities as controlled by both regional and national power dynamics regulated by laws of silence and behavior, and strengthened by the corruption and complicity of governmental and religious institutions. It also dwells on the cost of complying with codes of silence and buying into a corrupt system for individuals living in such realities.

The last three plays included in this volume make up *The Eyeglasses Trilogy* (2011), which includes *Holywater* (*Acquasanta*), *The Zisa Castle* (*Il castello della Zisa*), and *Dancers* (*Ballarini*). A multi-character monologue, *Holywater* recounts the tale of a land-bound homeless sailor, his loneliness, and his boundless love for the sea. *The Zisa Castle* is set in a Catholic care center for individuals with disabilities. The play sketches the daily routine of the two nuns who take care of Nicola, a catatonic young man. It posits questions of caretaking, compassion fatigue, and religious devotion as the play imagines what Nicola would say or do if he could wake up from his stupor and tell his own story. Finally, *Dancers* uses a detailed movement score and nostalgic Italian songs from the 1950s-1960s to capture the reunion of an old couple as they relive their love story backward in time.

Breathtakingly lyrical and painfully gut wrenching in their simplicity, these plays can be read as vehicles to denounce the symbolic and systemic violence targeting and oppressing both southern Italy and Italian women during the Berlusconi Era. Indeed, the topics the plays address – such as the disenfranchisement of the poor, gendered violence, and gender inequality – are still unmistakably relevant in today's Italy as they are in Trump's America. The lower-class Sicilian women in *The Trilogy of the Sicilian Family* are depicted as doubly marginalized by both their gender and socio-economic status. The *Trilogy* then renders visible how financial disparity between the sexes, assigned gender roles within families, and the violence perpetuated against women at the turn of the twenty-first century point at larger gender issues such as economic inequality, religion-backed ideas predicating "domestic feminism" and the submission of women to men, and gendered killings. *Market Dogs* denounces the complicity of the nation in helping the Sicilian mafia thrive. It utilizes female imagery to relate how southern Italian women living in mafia-controlled regions are perennially subordinated to men and marginalized within mafia organizations, where they are idealized by male fantasies and relegated to traditional gender roles. Lastly, while *The Eyeglasses Trilogy* as a whole focuses on the loneliness and disconnection of those living at the fringes of society, *Dancers* in particular raises pressing concerns about gendered ageism and the absence of older women's bodies, older women's sexuality, and the ageing process on stage and in the media. Overall the plays enlarge the conversation initiated by scholar Elaine Aston in her 2010 essay "Feeling the loss of feminism: Sarah Kane's Blasted and an Experiential Genealogy of Contemporary Women's Playwriting," regarding the state of feminist struggle in the theatre. They position Dante's work as interrogating the societal effects of a loss of feminism at the turn of the twenty-first century.

Navigating Bodies and Regional Languages: The Process of Translation

In a translator's note to an anthology of plays by contemporary Chilean playwright Juan Radrigán, *Finished from the Start and Other Plays*, Ana Elena Puga affirms that it is the translator's moral obligation, and, indeed, the moral duty of the whole production team tasked with bringing a work to life outside of its source culture, to embrace authors' indirect requests to "bear witness" to the suffering and history of their culture (xi). With my own translations, I want to bear witness to Dante's Sicilian and Southern Italian culture and to the social engagement at the heart of her work. Further, as a director and a scholar of Italian theatre, I wish to provide playable scripts of contemporary Italian plays in order to make the work of today's Italian women directors and playwrights more visible in English-language scholarship and on English-speaking stages. From these plays English-speaking readers and audiences may be able to glean a different, more complex image of Italy. They may look beyond Dante's metaphors to see a nation that is still socially and economically divided between North and South; a nation where women are still far from social and economic equality. They may also experience a theatre that speaks of the *Mezzogiorno*[1] and its issues; that exposes them to the mingling of multiple languages; that is able to let gestures and images speak louder than words.

Dante's plays pose an interesting dilemma when it comes to the task of translation. This is partly due to the mixture of languages present in the text and her emphasis on southern Italian languages, but also to the physical gestures that are often codified within the language itself and the physical devising process or *scrittura scenica* ('writing via staging' or 'staging to write') through which her works are created before becoming published scripts. Additionally, as author (and Dante's playwriting instructor at the Silvio D'Amico National Academy for the Dramatic Arts) Andrea Camilleri notes in his introduction to the Italian edition of the *Trilogy of the Sicilian Family*, each word that Dante utilizes is economical and precise, communicating to the viewer what needs to be said with immediacy. Hence, on the one hand, I wanted to preserve the complexity of the syntax, the leanness of her vocabulary, and rhythm of Dante's languages, the tensions between them, and the gestures and physicality embedded within them. On the other hand, I desired to render the text accessible to English-speaking readers and audiences. To negotiate these needs I drew on post-colonial translation theory, which proved useful primarily because of its emphasis on protecting minority cultures.

In addition to technical concerns such as syntax, punctuation, and rhythm, this approach considers the geographical and historical context of the original scripts. Protecting minority cultures is quite relevant when undertaking translations of Dante's plays since she permeates her work with the culture of a historically marginalized part of the Italian peninsula. Sicily – and, truly, most of the southern Italian peninsula as a whole – can be regarded as a post-colonial region in terms of its political, economic, and cultural development and of its historical, recurrent subjugation to foreign nations and other Italian kingdoms. In an attempt to identify and preserve the differences found in Sicilian culture, my translations make use of the ideas of Laurence Venuti, Susan Bassnett, Gayatri Chakravorty Spivak, and Kwame Anthony Appiah.

In *Scandals of Translation: Toward an Ethics of Difference* (1998) – as in all of his works – Venuti proposes a translation method bent on preserving what is "foreign" in the translated text. This process of "foreignizing" in order to respect a "minoratized" text contrasts with the process of "domestication," a method advocated by translators such as Suzanne Jill Levine. In *The Subversive Scribe: Translating Latin American Fiction* (1991), Levine views the translator as in charge of continuing the subversive work begun by authors in their own language. Levine believes that by subverting an author's text, the translator's work ultimately becomes part of a deconstructionist continuum that "already always alters the reality it intends to re-create" (Levine 8). This approach then justifies radical changes to a source text in translation under the pretense of a semiotics-based perpetual process of differ(e/a)nce and deferral for which even the source text is an adaptation of something that was already there.[2] When it comes to translating texts for the stage, this method is often supported with the rationale that, in order for a translation to be playable for the stage and enjoyable to its public, it must be palatable to the taste of and easily understood by the target audience. What this means is that translation is often sacrificed to adaptation. In this respect, the translation of Dario Fo's plays into English provide an interesting case study. As Joseph Farrell argues in his *Modern Drama* 1998 article "Variations on a Theme: Respecting Dario Fo," in order to subvert the text to render Fo's theatrical work more relevant to its audience abroad, many translators transformed his plays into English scripts that are only distantly related to the original text. As with other authors, this produced two authorial voices – an Italian one and a foreign one – shifting the engagement with the work from preoccupation with its political concerns to appreciation of its entertainment value. Those plays unceremoniously crossed the line from translation to adaptation, becoming so different from the original that they altered the perception of their author abroad. My aim for this anthology was to make sure that this would not happen to Dante's plays.

In order to create translations that allow future scholars to access this selection of Dante's texts and provide English-speaking companies with playable scripts, I undertook an in-depth textual and cultural analysis of the original plays. I sought to create scripts that, while still being accessible and engaging, also respected the political and sociological implications that surround a translation process sensitive to post-colonial theory. In doing so, I took an eclectic and pragmatic approach to Dante's scripts, adopting different strategies to favor a "foreignizing" translation while contemplating the 'totality' of her work as presented on the page, treating stage directions and descriptions in the text with as much attention as the dialogue itself.

As the plays in this collection are translated into English from marginalized cultures, languages, and/or social groups from post-colonial regions, I felt it imperative to account for the power dynamics that surround the translation of these plays into a colonizing culture as Susan Bassnett suggests in "Of Colonies, Cannibals and Vernaculars" (1999) and *Translation Studies* (2002). I wanted to resist a "domesticating" approach and possible cultural appropriation. I was also conscious of the risk, pointed at by Bassnett, but also by Spivak and Appiah, of homogenizing the minority cultures present in Dante's play into a unified, indistinct field of Otherness subjugated to a central, Anglophone Subject that did not account for gender and cultural differentiation. Thus, I set to created what Venuti called a "foreignizing language:" a heterogeneous language of my own that would remind readers and audiences that they are dealing with a text in translation, originally written in another language and for another audience.

To stylistically address the entirety of Dante's own complex, crossbred language, it did not seem appropriate to use American English as a base language and English dialects, such as an Italian-American standardized dialect, to signal regional color and class. Specifically, I opted not to adopt traditional Italian-Americanisms or linguistic idiosyncrasies usually associated with Italian immigrants for two reasons. Firstly, I felt that such course of action would have conflated the very Sicilian and Neapolitan characters of the anthology with existing stereotypical images of Italian immigrants to the United States. Secondly, I resisted the notion of relocating these characters onto American soil. Since I aimed to preserve the plays' own cultural identity and their political connotations, I wanted to keep the plays set in Sicily. Thus, like Dante had done in the original plays, I strived to create a hybrid language to let the audience encounter foreign words and concepts expressed in Sicilian, Neapolitan, Italian, and French.

In *Holywater*, my desire for such a language presents itself in the word 'ppocundria'. As untranslatable as the Portuguese word 'saudade', the Neapolitan 'ppocundria' expresses a lethargic, apathetic helplessness and longing. As the audience can piece the meaning of the word together from the context in which it is used, it seemed appropriate to leave it – and the aloofness of its exact meaning – in its original language. This choice demands that the readers as well as the audience meet the translation half-way, moving closer to the source text and culture instead of demanding that the text move closer to them. This is a necessary act to protect and maintain in translation the differences found in minority cultures and as, Spivak asserts in her 1992 essay "The Politics of Translation," to renegotiate the audience's positionality with respect to the original and translated text.

Furthermore, in an attempt to be true to my desire to create "foreignized" scripts, I took care not to generalize Dante's characters as Italians and to preserve their regional identity by keeping their proper names and the places in which they dwell in their original Italian, Sicilian or Neapolitan. Additionally, I kept intact the original Sicilian and Neapolitan manipulations of characters' proper names to express endearment. For example, in *The Butchery*, the brothers use the diminutive 'Ninuzza' to address their sister Nina. Adding the suffix 'uzza' or 'uzzo' to a noun (proper or otherwise) is a Sicilian convention to express affection for something or someone lovely. In the case of individuals, it also marks them as young or even childish as it can be seen in *The Butchery* where the brothers often use 'Ninuzza' to patronize and control their sister. Preserving the shift from 'Nina' to 'Ninuzza' signals and linguistically complements the brothers' behavioral shifts, which are central to the play's atmosphere of violence and to the menacing development of the male characters' ferocity toward their sister.

In the context of creating a hybrid language for these translations, the title of *Carnezzeria*, the second play of the trilogy, posed a particularly difficult challenge. Here I took literally Venuti's injunction to invent a new language to suit translation needs. The word 'carnezzeria' is a word that is only used in the dialect of the Sicilian language spoken in Palermo and can be roughly translated as 'meat shop.' Significantly, Dante elected to use 'carnezzeria' instead of the Italian word 'macelleria,' in order to underline the fundamental themes of the play. In fact, by using a word that incorporates 'carne' (meat), attention is immediately redirected to the body as meat and to the body's primal, animalistic instincts and desires, such as violence and sex. Focus is also drawn to another Italian word: 'carneficina' (slaughter) with its bloody, raw implications much less neat and sterile than those implied by the word 'macelleria.' In translating the Palermitan word 'carnezzeria,' I opted to preserve such connotations by electing to use 'butchery' (meaning slaughterhouse). Of British origin, thus already unfamiliar to American ears, this word helps establish a sense of "foreignness" before the beginning of the play. 'Butchery' retains connotations of a 'wanton, indiscriminate, and cruel killing,' 'slaughter,' or 'carnage.' Further, the word is used in slang to signify something 'botched' or 'handled badly.' While it does trade the emphasis on meat with a focus on those who carry out its butchering, the word retains a double connotation that strays away from a specific physical location (a meat shop, a butcher shop, or a slaughterhouse) to point at the locale of a possible 'badly handled slaughter,' thus capitalizing on the raw feeling given out by the word 'carnezzeria.' Further, the relative dimensions of a butchery as compared to a slaughterhouse helped to keep the play confined to the original contained domestic sphere of Dante's play: whereas 'butchery' may evoke the image of a mom-and-pop's shop, 'slaughterhouse' could also evoke a large, industrial establishment where systematic killing occurs. In the context of the familial gender politics of the play, translating *Carnezzeria* as *The Butchery* then allows for a much stronger political commentary. At the same time, it steers clear from reminding the audience of slasher films or unintentional references to the Kurt Vonnegut novel *Slaughterhouse-Five* and its many adaptations.

As a way to destabilize the language-power relationships that necessarily emerge when the works of minority cultures are translated into another (often colonialist or neo-colonialist) language, in these scripts Sicilian, Neapolitan, and Italian are mixed within an American English that is often subverted in its own syntactic structure (frequently rendering it grammatically incorrect) to follow, for example, the rhythm and the cadence of Italian regional speech. This strategy preserves some of the tension created by Dante in juxtaposing the languages present in the original scripts. For instance, in the third play of *The Trilogy of the Sicilian Family*, the Mother refers to her sons as '*vita mia*,' ending a large number of her sentences with this very Sicilian construct that can be translated as 'my life.' In Dante's work, using the regional '*a vita mia*' instead of the Italian '*la mia vita*,' underlines the word 'vita' or 'life' to focus on the Mother's life but also on her life's absolute dependence on that of her children's. To preserve this turn of phrase's complex meaning, I chose to use a more literal translation for this expression, which, incidentally, doubles as the title of the play. This process of selective literal translation or "thick translation," as Appiah names it in his homonymous 1993 essay, invites the audience to consider different views of the world and challenges them to understand another culture's complex ways of communication. Hence, to retain 'life' as the powerful, central focus of this phrase's English translation, to maintain its playful ambiguity, and to preserve the poetic tone of the original Sicilian for an English-speaking audience, I used the "thick" translation 'life of mine.'

In these scripts I also labored to preserve the register and power shifts in the dialogue present in the original texts when characters switch from a regional language to Italian. Sometimes, purposefully non-translated dialectal words signal these shifts. Other times, an overly polite, formal, and even stiff English stands in for Dante's use of Italian to express an affected cultural superiority or to mock characters – something that can be seen throughout *The Butchery* and *Market Dogs*.

In this collection, I resisted the urge to add too many explanatory endnotes since a play should stand on its own when staged, as David Johnston makes clear in *Stages of Translation* (1996). Nonetheless, I provided endnote translations of the words, phrases, and larger portions of text that were left in their original language – such as parts of Zia Lucia's monologue about "going out in Italian" in *mPalermu* or the monologue that the older nun delivers in French in *The Zisa Castle*. Additionally, endnotes provide the necessary dramaturgical context to understand obscure cultural references such as those to the songs included in *Holywater* and *Dancers*, or to a particular soccer team or players in *mPalermu* and *Life of Mine*. In the latter case, although the explicit references in both plays would be unfamiliar to most people in the United States, the specific actions that Dante's stage directions call for, in conjunction with the dialogue associated with those references, would contextualize them for the audience.

Working always with the *mise-en-scène* in mind, as Johnston suggests, I devoted particular attention to preserving implicit references to gestures and the body that, although easily understood by both Italian actors and audiences, need to be decoded for English-speaking theatre practitioners and foreign audiences. The word 'Nzuú' found in *mPalermu* is one such example. 'Nzuú' is an onomatopoeic word pronounced as a palato-alveolar click that functions as a signifier for both 'no' and a particular gesture that indicates negation. This gesture accompanies the sound and quickly brings the tongue to the hard palate while the top of the head inclines backward and the chin is brought forward before being restored to a neutral position. Directors who would like to preserve the meaning and movement associated with 'Nzuú' should find the endnote helpful.

The steps in the concretization of the reception of a play in translation are only fully realized when the play is received as a performance by an audience in the target culture – something that Patrice Pavis aptly observes in his 1992 "Toward Specifying Theatre Translation." This is especially important when it comes to translations of Dante's plays. In fact, the play's scripts result from a long devising process that relies on the body and its physicality as an essential component to express socio-political realities. The translations here anthologized benefitted from a series of staged readings at The Ohio State University. Further, in May 2014, *Dancers* was staged as a workshop production directed by Shelby Brewster and performed by Sifiso Mazibuko and Sarah Ware. The play's abundant dance numbers, stylized movement sequences, and sentimental love songs coupled with minimal dialogue made it easily accessible to non-Italian speaking audiences and, in May 2015, *Dancers* was fully produced under my direction, starring Sifiso Mazibuko, Sarah Ware, and the lighting of Alex Kyle-Dipietropaolo. *Dancers* had its English language premier in July 2015 at The Courtyard Theatre in London as part of Palindrome Productions' 2015 season. In August of that same year it was remounted for the New York Fringe Festival. Audiences and critics alike received the piece enthusiastically. An audience member observed: "[Dancers is] Profound. A fugue. Deep like the memories of a past love [...] Ironic, heart wrenching, nostalgic, and joyful. It touches you deep, it moves you, it makes you smile. It breaks your heart." In her review of the piece, New York-based critic Alison Durkee wrote: "*Dancers* has a weight to its simplicity that makes it not only an engaging performance, but a genuinely moving journey."

It is my sincere hope that these translations will enable English-speaking theatre scholars, directors, and readers alike to have many fruitful, moving encounters with Emma Dante's theatre.

Works Cited

Appiah, Kwame Anthony. "Thick Translation." *The Translation Studies Reader*. 3rd ed. Ed. Lawrence Venuti. New York: Routledge, 2012. (331-343).

Aston, Elaine. "Feeling the Loss of Feminism: Sarah Kane's 'Blasted' and an Experiential Genealogy of Contemporary Women's Playwriting." *Theatre Journal* 62.4 (2010): 575–591.

Bassnett, Susan. *Translation Studies*. New York: Routledge, 2002.

---, and Harish Trivedi. "Of colonies, cannibals and vernaculars." *Post-colonial Translation: Theory and Practice*. London: Routledge, 1999.

Comparozzi, Alessandra. Review of Dancers at FringeNYC. *Facebook*. 26 August 2015, https://www.facebook.com/alessandra.comparozzi/posts/10204988463446435. Accessed 11 May 2017.

Durkee, Alison. "FringeNYC Review: Dancers." *Stagebuddy.com*. 22 August 2015, https://stagebuddy.com/dance/dance-review/fringenyc-review-dancers. Accessed 11 May 2017.

Farrell, Joseph. "Variations on a Theme: Respecting Dario Fo." *Modern Drama*. 41.1 (1998).

Johnston, David. *Stages of Translation*. Bath, England: Absolute Classics, 1996.

Levine, Suzanne J. *The Subversive Scribe: Translating Latin American Fiction*. Saint Paul, Minn: Graywolf Press, 1991.

Pavis, Patrice. "Towards Specifying Theatre Translation." *Theatre at the Crossroads of Culture*. London: Routledge, 1992. 131-154.

Puga, Ana Elena. "Translator's Note." *Finished from the Start and Other Plays*. Juan Radrigán, Trans. Ana E. Puga with Mónica Núñez-Parra. Evanston, Ill: Northwestern University Press, 2007. xi-xxvi.

Spivak, Gayatri Chakravorty. "The Politics of Translation." *The Translation Studies Reader.* 3rd ed. Ed. Lawrence Venuti. New York: Routledge, 2012. 312-330.

Venuti, Lawrence. *The Scandals of Translation: Towards an Ethics of Difference.* London: Routledge, 1998.

The Trilogy of the Sicilian Family

◆

mPalermu

The Butchery

Life of Mine

mPalermu

◆

"There are moments when the truth reveals itself completely to our eyes, without our having to make a gesture, take a step, move an eyelash. I saw that sea now illuminated by a winter sun, a sea azure and remote among sparse and motionless ships; I saw, as if I were not in that carriage, but in another place, in the air – I saw what was in their eyes; now that the ship rested empty in the harbor, and far, almost hopeless, appeared the hour of a new voyage – the deaf regret of having already consumed almost all one's existence, having unwound the yarn up to the last piece of thread."[3]

— ANNA MARIA ORTESE
from "Arrivo a Palermo"
in *Il mormorio di Parigi*

Palermo. If it had a body, it'd use it to dodge. What? Everything. To not be hit, identified. The emblem, the crest on its shield is silence. *mPalermu* speaks of this silence, of this immobility that is, from a close distance, familial. Of indoors and outdoors divided by a threshold that is impossible to cross. Of gestures that are perfectly formed in the mind, but that can't get through to the muscles, to the blood, like children eternally nourished by ever-pregnant mothers but never birthed.

    mPalermu means inside Palermo. It is a fertile womb, where too many children huddle in the dark alleys of its deformed abdomen, and while they suck lymph from a tangle of umbilical cords, they kick, they push but they don't want to get out.

    In Palermo no actions are taken, rather ceremonies are staged; no dialogues take place, rather people operate rhetorically by citing, winking, alluding… it is the city of waste and the superfluous, of magnificent decorations crowning dilapidation.

    This theater of the impossible, which makes of Palermo a kind of symbolic representation of the soul of the world, incessantly busy and incessantly dying, is our *commedia*.

— EMMA DANTE

mPalermu, winner of the 2001 Scenario Prize and the 2002 UBU Award, was first staged in Parma at the Teatro del Parco in November 2001, in a production by Compagnia Sud Costa Occidentale directed by Emma Dante.

    The people who performed this play are Gaetano Bruno (Mimmo), Tania Garribba (Grandma Citta), Sabino Civilleri (Giammarco), Italia Carroccio (the first Aunt Lucia), Ersilia Lombardo (the last Aunt Lucia), and Manuela Lo Sicco (Rosalia). Without them this story would have never been written.

The CAROLLO Family lined up on the proscenium line.

From left to right:
MIMMO
GRANDMA CITTA[4]
GIAMMARCO
AUNT LUCIA
ROSALIA

From right to left:
ROSALIA
AUNT LUCIA
GIAMMARCO
GRANDMA CITTA
MIMMO

The Awakening

From darkness to light, in slow progression, during the giaculatorias.[5]

VOICES:
Hey, are we opening up this window?
Hey, can't you see? It's daybreak!
Rosalia, hey, can't you hear me calling you?
Rosalia?
Hey, can't you hear?
Chi duluri![6]
Even grandma woke up!
I can't find my shirt with the white collar!
Father, son, and holy spirit, it's daybreak!
Hey, are you getting me my shirt or not?
Mimmo?
It hurts!
Outside there aaaaaare really amazing things!
Open the window and look:
the sun's out! It's real beautiful... Have a taste!
Have a taste!

Five actors on stage. Five conjoint relatives, all obedient to this law marked onto them. A family: MIMMO *the most authoritative,* GRANDMA CITTA *the old woman from Pollena Trocchia (in the province of Naples) who emigrated south,* GIAMMARCO *the distantly related parasite,* AUNT LUCIA *an unmarried young mother, and* ROSALIA *married to Alfonso who works up north.*
Five actors who are a family, and we who watch them.

11

It's Sunday morning. The Carollo family is lined up at the front door and is getting ready to go out. A few rays of sunshine filter in through the blinds. The five relatives, excited, toss each other clothes while they chatter loudly. They are poor and, besides the rags they gaily put on, they own only a large plastic container filled to the brim with water and the individually gift-wrapped pastry they each clutch in their hands. MIMMO whistles, happy. He, together with the others, has one task: to act. To cross the threshold, to put one foot in front of the other and go. Outside. In the streets. To walk with their head held high. To each pad their soul so that it won't fly away as the door opens wide. To invent lies to screw the feeling of senselessness that overcomes us when faced with every gesture. Everything is ready, in a bit they'll go out and to hell with whoever lowers their gaze: there's no shame, no guilt. The dignity of the Carollos is the crown of kings. The relatives sneer, mock each other, but also proudly admire one another.

ROSALIA:
Come on, should we go out?

MIMMO:
E certo che dobbiamo uscire![7]

AUNT LUCIA (*whispering to* ROSALIA):
He said it in Italian!

MIMMO:
Why, what is it?

AUNT LUCIA:
Nothing…

MIMMO:
Ah, it seemed like you were making fun of me!

AUNT LUCIA:
Would I ever…?

ROSALIA:
Let's go out!

MIMMO:
But not with those slippers, Rosalia!

They all stare at ROSALIA's *light blue slippers and, blushing, they turn toward us. Silence falls.* ROSALIA, *all dressed up, has kept on her slippers.* MIMMO, *bothered by the gaze of the audience, glues his eyes onto* ROSALIA.

ROSALIA:
What have they got to do with anything?

MIMMO:
Precisely, they've got nothing to do with it. Take off those slippers and put on a pair of shoes like everyone else, let's go!

He nervously whistles while he waits.

ROSALIA:
Why should I take them off? I'm not barefoot!

MIMMO:
You're not barefoot, true, but you've got to take those slippers off, now! I don't want to argue, Rosalia.

ROSALIA (*suddenly turning toward an audience member*):
What are you looking at?

Pause

GRANDMA CITTA:
Chi duluri!

MIMMO:
Whore of an Eve, Rosalia, why do you have to make me angry?

ROSALIA:
Why, are you dressed?

MIMMO (*suddenly turning toward an audience member*):
What are you looking at?

Pause

AUNT LUCIA:
Come on, Rosalia, put on your shoes!

GIAMMARCO (*to* MIMMO):
Did you see your pants?

Suddenly, everyone turns toward MIMMO *to focus on a detail: his pants are so rundown that a beggar wouldn't take them even if they were a present. From the corner of his eye,* GIAMMARCO *examines* MIMMO. *He keeps close guard. He senses in the air the usual quiet before the storm.*

MIMMO (*to* GRANDMA CITTA *who stands between him and* GIAMMARCO):
Grandma Citta, move over a bit!

GRANDMA CITTA *moves.*

14

Giammarco can't see me well yet, grandma, move another little bit!

GRANDMA CITTA *takes another little step backward.*

Thank you!!! (*To* GIAMMARCO, *challenging*) Giammarco, now that you can see me fully, tell me: what's wrong with these pants?

GIAMMARCO:
They're short!

ROSALIA:
Short!

MIMMO:
How are they? I didn't quite hear you!

GIAMMARCO:
Tight!

ROSALIA:
Tight!

MIMMO:
But, who asked you?

GIAMMARCO (*pointing at* ROSALIA):
I'm her brother-in-law!

ROSALIA:
My husband's brother!

MIMMO:
And who are you to me?

GIAMMARCO (*pointing at* ROSALIA):
I'm still her brother-in-law, no?

MIMMO:
Quite right!

GIAMMARCO:
And he, her husband, who is also my brother, blood of my blood, begged nothing else of me: fight tooth and nail to defend Rosalia…

MIMMO (*referring to the pastry in his hand*):
You see this pastry?

GIAMMARCO:
Se.[8]

MIMMO:
As soon as I put this pastry on the floor and finally free my hands, I'll take off my belt and break it over your head. You got anything else to add?

GIAMMARCO:
You even have pink socks that make you look like a bon bon.

ROSALIA:
Bon bon!

MIMMO (*puts the pastry on the floor*):
And, meanwhile, I'll put this down!

GIAMMARCO (*Shivering, he puts down his pastry, accepting the challenge.*):
And I'll put it down too, let's go! You think I'm scared of you?

MIMMO (*taking off the belt from his trousers*):
And, meanwhile, I'll take this off!

16

AUNT LUCIA:
No, Mimmo, leave him be!!!

MIMMO:
Silence! I've got plenty for everyone, you lousy bunch! I'll pound you! Useless things! You're one worse than the other. You don't deserve anything!

AUNT LUCIA (*screaming*):
No! Mimmo!!!

MIMMO is furious. He doesn't feel pity for anyone. Cracking his whip, he marks out a path for AUNT LUCIA, GIAMMARCO, ROSALIA, *and* GRANDMA CITTA *who, biting the bullet, perform their circus numbers. Standing in the middle of the ring,* MIMMO *is the circus tamer who makes his animals jump. He hunts them, wounds them, and, lost in a delirium of hate and love, asks for their forgiveness.*

Lashes of Love

MIMMO (*while he whips them*):
I'll kill you, son of bitches, I'll slaughter you!
Don't look at me, you bastards, don't criticize me. Ever! (*With tenderness*)
Is this how you thank me, Rosalia? Give me a kiss, come on! What would
that cost you? Don't make me angry! A kiss, Rosalia, and everything is
fixed! Grandma Citta, let me rest my head in your lap, and hold me!
Tight, though! Aunt Lucia, you tell them! I love you! Why, when you tell
me to do something, don't I do it?
I do everything for you, everything! Come on, Aunt Lucia, that I care
for you. I love all of you. Even you Giammarco, come here! Don't leave
me alone like a dog, that I love you. I swear it's true! (*Aggressively*) But
why do you look at me like that, son of a cocksucker? Don't look at me,
you bastards, don't criticize me. Ever! Because otherwise I'll kill you, I'll
slaughter you!!! Rotters, I'll crush you into dust…

MIMMO *cracks the whip with all the strength he has until, exhausted, he falls
to the ground.* AUNT LUCIA *fixes her dress and, as per an immutable rite
that keeps repeating itself, she helps him stand up. Then, as if nothing had
happened, she moves her head slightly, inviting the others to go back in line in
front of the door.*
MIMMO *comes forward, menacing, and, whistling, puts the belt back on.*

MIMMO:
Come on, let's go out! Come on!

Pause

AUNT LUCIA (*pointing at* ROSALIA'*s slippers, terrified*):
With those slippers?

Pause

MIMMO:
Yes, with those slippers!

Pause

GIAMMARCO (*pointing at* MIMMO'*s trousers, terrified*):
With those short pants?

ROSALIA:
Shorts?

Pause

MIMMO (*trying to keep calm*):
My pants are not short!

GIAMMARCO:
They're short, Mimmo! Look closely and see for yourself.

AUNT LUCIA:
Don't get mad, Mimmo, there's nothing wrong with them! They fit you well, listen to me!

MIMMO (*to* GRANDMA CITTA):
Are they short?

GRANDMA CITTA:
N'anticchièdda![9]

GIAMMARCO:
More than a little!

MIMMO:
First off, she said a little!

GIAMMARCO:
And, meanwhile, I tell you it's more than a little!

GRANDMA CITTA *laughs quietly and smacks her purse against her legs, so to be noticed by* MIMMO.

GIAMMARCO (*pointing at* GRANDMA CITTA):
See, she's laughing!

MIMMO:
Leave her alone, she's not laughing.

GIAMMARCO:
But she's laughing her ass off!

MIMMO:
Grandma, don't you start too!

GRANDMA CITTA *laughs harder and involves* MIMMO. *The tension fades. Everyone laughs and they are restored to their initial happy and lively selves.*

GIAMMARCO:
It's right for grandma to laugh, Mimmuzzo.[10] What: first you raised stinking hell, and now we have to go out with these short pants and with these slippers? But where are we going, Mimmo? You're ridiculous dressed like that!

MIMMO *(laughing at* GIAMMARCO's *line)*:
Why, did you take a look at your jacket from the Great War?

GIAMMARCO:
So what? Aren't we still in the postwar era?

MIMMO:
Yes, but not of the first. We've already had a second.

GIAMMARCO:
And if they do a third?

MIMMO:
We'll hear the boom!!!

They almost split their sides with laughter.

AUNT LUCIA:
Handsome you are, both of you! Did you have to go through this charade? Always making me worry myself sick!

MIMMO:
What, was it all my fault, Aunt Lucia?

ROSALIA *bursts into a hysteric laugh.*

Rosalia of the Slippers

ROSALIA:

No, it's my fault! Because I don't have shoes! (*She hands her purse to* AUNT LUCIA.) Sorry, can you pass it to Giammarco? Giammarco, can you pass it to Grandma? Grandma, can you hand it to your grandson? Mimmo can you hold it for me? (MIMMO *takes the purse.*) There's nothing inside, I don't need it. And besides, what am I going to do with a purse if I don't have shoes? (*Accusing* MIMMO) You didn't want to buy me shoes! I told him I needed them, but he didn't want to buy them for me! And now I'm going to show you how one goes out into the streets wearing slippers! I'll do a demonstration for you: this is the street! (*She walks back and forth, swaying her hips and dragging the slippers.*) This is how you go out into the streets with slippers! Dancing dancing! Are they looking at me? (*She points at the slippers.*) They light up! You can see them even in the dark! Wait, I'll ask them: (*to an audience member*) you mister, pardon me, good man, do you think the blue of my slippers goes well with the pink of my blouse? Careful! For me, it doesn't! It doesn't! I've got to change to go out! (*She starts to undress.*) I've got to put on something that matches these slippers! I don't know, fuchsia panties! I've got to fix myself up to go out, right? It's not like I can go out like this! I have to make myself beautiful, elegant, like all the others.
(*She pulls up her slip and points at her panties.*) Do these go? Do these match the slippers, huh? Can we go out like this? Let's go out! I'm ready! (*She walks back and forth, sashaying with her slip pulled up.*) I'm Mimmo's cousin!

ROSALIA *takes off her slip and unhooks her bra with the intention of provoking a scandal.* MIMMO *and* AUNT LUCIA *fling themselves onto her to cover her up.* GIAMMARCO *drags* GRANDMA CITTA *to the font of the stage and, to hide his shame, tells her and the audience an anecdote from his one and only trip outside Palermo.*

The Cities of Foni and Pollena Trocchia
Or
Giammarco and Grandma Citta on the Road

GIAMMARCO (*awkwardly, to the audience*):
I once went on a trip to a city called Foni. I don't remember where it is,
but I remember that, to go there, I had to take the train... and nothing!
When I got to the station, an old pal of my brother Alfonso who works
up north, was waiting for me. He has a small house in Foni but a very airy
one, because it has nice big windows and you can breathe in nice fresh
air... Oh!... Foni is too beautiful, folks! You want to know why?
Because it has a big square and when you walk through it your heart
opens up, because the pavement is nice and smooth and you don't have to
watch where you put your feet, am I right?
No tripping. It's a good thing for you, Grandma Citta, since you always
wear stilettos... what was I telling you? Ah! Foni's square! In the middle
of this big square there's a long pole and what's on top of this long pole?
The statue of a fellow with a beard who's laughing and holding out a hand
scrunched in a fist.
I asked a young fellow who was passing by: "Excuse me but, what did this
statue hold in its hand before: a flower? A candle? Or an ice-cream cone?"
"Nossir," he answered: "This statue held power in its hand!" Look at that,
power! Could it ever be that it held power in its hand? Who's he, the
Almighty? Then I looked at him more closely and he looked like Mimmo,
and a lot too.
The precise, identical, spitting image of that beanpole of Mimmo.

MIMMO *gets back in the line*

He was your spitting image, Mimmuzzo! But don't get mad. Listen here: while I was looking at him, I saw that a small pigeon, flapping and flying, sat on top of the fist and shat on it and I fucking died laughing! There were so many pigeons in that square that went to shit inside the statue's fist. People gave them food: bread, cookies, chocolates, and the little pigeons shat. I gave them food too: bread, tiny cookies, chocolates, I even gave them ice-cream and the pigeons pecked at it a whole lot.
They pecked, Grandma Citta, I gave them food and they pecked... then I looked at my watch and I saw it was late and I had to leave, am I right Rosalia?

ROSALIA, *accompanied by* AUNT LUCIA *and dressed like in the beginning, gets back in the line.*

I started to walk, handsome, elegant, and smug as I am. But, while I walked something really strange happened, folks: the pigeons began to chase me and they pecked at my head, I ran and they pecked... they pecked... and I thought: see? If only Mimmo was here! If Mimmo was there, that day, we'd have eaten pigeons!

MIMMO (*He laughs.*):
If I was there I'd have clobbered them to death!

GIAMMARCO:
You'd crack their heads and we'd have roasted and eaten them!

MIMMO:
For sure! Do you think I don't like roasted pigeons?

Pause
They all look at each other, full of hope, waiting for MIMMO*'s word.*

Now, can we go out?

Pause

GIAMMARCO:
Let's go out!

MIMMO:
Give this bag to Rosalia!

GIAMMARCO:
There, wretch. You almost gave me a heart attack!

GRANDMA CITTA (*to an audience member*):
When I was young, I was beautiful!

MIMMO:
What, are you ugly now? (*To* AUNT LUCIA) As soon as she feels over-looked because we're focusing on something else, she instantly livens up. (*To* GRANDMA CITTA) You're still beautiful, Grandma Citta. You hear? Beautiful! I'd kiss her all over this one, mark my words! (*He kisses her on the head.*)

GRANDMA CITTA:
I walked, and walked, and everyone looked at me...

MIMMO:
Ya, ok!

GRANMA CITTA:
I lived very far away.

MIMMO:
Grab that duffle bag and let's go out, Grandma Citta! Let's go!

GRANMA CITTA:
I lived on the mainland…

GIAMMARCO:
It's begun…

GRANMA CITTA:
I lived in a big city called Pollena Trocchia.

MIMMO:
Of course!

GRANMA CITTA:
Pollena Trocchia is its name, 'cause its two villages…

EVERYONE (*chorus-like*):
…but the parish is the same.

MIMMO:
We know it by heart, am I right?

GIAMMARCO:
You've told us this story a thousand times, Grandma Citta! The sky's going to get dark like this! We have to go out…

GRANMA CITTA:
When I was little…

GIAMMARCO:
Stop her, folks, otherwise she'll go off like a rocket…

GRANMA CITTA:
…I always used to go inside that church and I also went to the sanctuary that's close by.

MIMMO:
Stop, grandma, we've got to go out…

GRANMA CITTA:
A huge sanctuary…

GIAMMARCO:
The 500 is off!

GRANDMA CITTA:
…huge, huge, huge…

GIAMMARCO:
She's going to do a heel and toe, look! Take away her license!

GRANMA CITTA:
…even bigger than the cathedral of Palermo…

Pause

GIAMMARCO:
What did you say?

GRANMA CITTA:
The sanctuary of Pollena Trocchia is bigger than the cathedral of Palermo!

Pause

GIAMMARCO:
That's new! Who told her that crap?

They all look at each other in silence.

GIAMMARCO:
It can't be, dear granny! It must be a mistake. Because Palermo's cathedral is bigger than the sanctuary of Polly an' a Troyka, right? Go on…

GRANMA CITTA:
The sanctuary of Pollena Trocchia…

Pause

GRANMA CITTA:
…which is not smaller than the cathedral of Palermo…

GIAMMARCO:
Then you don't hear well, dear granny, let me explain it again.
Turn on your hearing aid 'cause I'm giving you the headline: THE CATHEDRAL OF PALERMO IS BIGGER THAN THE SANCTUARY OF POLLY AN' A TROYKA. Understood?

MIMMO:
But what the fuck do you care? Say yes! Put your head down, so we'll get out!

GIAMMARCO:
Ah, I should be a shitty sludge like you, right? Grandma Citta, listen to me: that treasonous crook of your nephew Mimmo, told me to pretend you're right!

MIMMO:
I didn't say anything, you're nothing but a liar…

ROSALIA:
Let's do this!

GIAMMARCO:
What?

ROSALIA:
They're the same size!

Pause

GIAMMARCO:
Whore of an Eve, Rosalia, they're not the same! Why? Because it's common knowledge all over the world that the cathedral of Palermo is bigger than the sanctuary of Pollyanatroyka. (*To* GRANDMA CITTA) Go on…

GRANMA CITTA:
It's bigger because it's up north!

ROSALIA:
It could be, that Grandma Citta's right, because when my husband writes me from up north, he always tells me: Rosalia, here everything is much bigger!

GRANMA CITTA:
Big, big, huge, the sanctuary of Pollena Trocchia is so big, but so big that it contains all the cathedrals in the world…

GIAMMARCO:
Hold on! You're right, dear granny! It's true: the cathedral of Palermo is the same size as the sanctuary of Pollyanatroyka, right? But… Palermo is in Serie A! (*To* MIMMO, *excited*) Isn't it right, sludge?

MIMMO:
Right, smench!

GIAMMARCO:
Do you remember the last match?

MIMMO:
Why, wasn't I sitting in the Curva Nord?

GIAMMARCO:
Palermo vs Triestina

MIMMO:
And who was it that passed the ball?

GIAMMARCO:
Gasbarroni?

ROSALIA:
Filippini!

GIAMMARCO:
Right, Filippini!

MIMMO:
And who scored?

GIAMMARCO:
Uncle Toni!

MIMMO:
I remember that play: Filippini took the ball and crossed it to him...

MIMMO, *shouting like a madman, retells the Palermo vs Triestina soccer game that immortalized the Palermo soccer team in Serie A.*

MIMMO:
Toni stops the ball, puts it on his head, and he looks at it with both eyes so much so that he almost becomes a little cross-eyed. He was so fabulous he looked like a seal… He was so good they called him Cabubi.[11] (*He imitates a seal.*) Arf, arf, arf!!! He puts the ball on his shoulders, he puts it on his belly, he lets it slip onto his feet and puts it here, there, up, and down… Down on the right and on the left, on the right and on the left, he stops it, he passes it to this guy, he passes it to this other guy, nutmegs the opponent, he looses his marker, he stops the ball and passes it to another guy…

The Ball's Dance

Everyone seems to have gone mad: they lay their pastries on the ground and, while in a line, they start to mime the game like real football-fanatics, kicking an imaginary ball. The dribbles, the crosses, the feints, and the goals of the Carollos make eyes turn. The ball bounces and all hell breaks loose.

MIMMO (*throwing* ROSALIA *the ball*):
Boom! He didn't understand anything anymore because he had this thick layer of dust all over his face and he remembered when he was little and his father used to tell him: "Look, if you don't study I won't let you go to Sunday School." But in that moment, he thought: "I don't give a shit, now I make the rules." And he passed the ball to another guy…

ROSALIA *passes the ball to* AUNT LUCIA.

He was a phenomenon! They called him "Maradona" because, with all that footwork he'd never let you realize where the ball was.

AUNT LUCIA *bounces the ball with her hands and* MIMMO, *angry, addresses* GIAMMARCO.

What the fuck is she doing? Take that ball away from her!!!! Take that ball away, Giammarco!!!

AUNT LUCIA, *amused, passes the ball from one hand to the other.*

Aunt Lucia, not like that, that's basketball… No, but what are you doing, it's insulting! Pass the ball to Giammarco, come on! This game isn't for girls, Aunt Lucia!

AUNT LUCIA *throws the ball to* GIAMMARCO.

Giammarco, pass me that ball! Pass me that ball or I'll slaughter you! I'll show you how it's played… Pass me that fucking ball Giammarco!!!

Keeping in line, the team backs up and follows the trajectory of the ball. MIMMO *winds up to kick and smashes the ball: the ball bounces off* GIAMMARCO's *butt and hits the forehead of* GRANDMA CITTA *who stretches up and pulls down to head-butt it but the ball can't be stopped, not even with grenades: one, two, three, four, five, six, seven, eight, nine… she looks like a pinball machine.*
The three players exchange places and attack in midfield. AUNT LUCIA *sings the Italian national anthem while* ROSALIA, *wearing her slippers, tries to catch the ball to keep it from crossing the goal line and scoring a gooooal. They're possessed, these world champions. The ball is alive and, crazy with happiness, it bounces, it falls down, it goes up, it slides along their backs, it rolls between their legs, it twirls, it takes off, it glides… the ball dances, it whirls on their bodies and when it flies off a window, the players go back to lining up along the proscenium, and, lifting their gaze to the sky, they notice the full moon.*

ROSALIA:
Look, it flew away!

Pause

AUNT LUCIA:
It's late!

Pause

MIMMO:
Should we go out?

GIAMMARCO:
Let's go out!

Quickly, everyone picks up their pastry from the front of the stage.

MIMMO (*noticing that* GIAMMARCO *has his package*):
Give me my pastry, Giammarco!

GIAMMARCO (*pointing at the package in* MIMMO's *hands*):
Isn't that your pastry, Mimmuzzo?

MIMMO:
No. (*Pointing at the package in* GIAMMARCO's *hands with his finger*) It's this one!

GIAMMARCO:
You're wrong: that's your pastry and this is my pastry! Rosalia, spruce up that Louis XIV bow and let's go, it's getting late!

MIMMO:
Freeze, Rosa!
Giammarco, I'm telling you that it's the one you're holding in your hands;
that's my pastry!

GIAMMARCO:
No, Mimmo, you airhead: this is my pastry and that one you have in your
hands is your pastry. Rosalia, shift into four-wheel drive and let's clear
out!

MIMMO:
You move, I'll slaughter you! First point: you're the airhead. Second
point: where did you get this pastry?

GIAMMARCO (*pointing somewhere near* MIMMO's *slippers*):
Here!

MIMMO:
And my slippers, the ones I took off before, when I put on my shoes, they
are here, aren't they?

GIAMMARCO:
That's right!

MIMMO:
So, you now find yourself in my spot, correct? And therefore the pastry
is mine!

GIAMMARCO:
No, Mimmuzzo, the slippers are yours, but the pastry, that is mine.
Rosalia, gang, let's move!

MIMMO:
Stop there, Rosa!
But why, Giammarco, you, before, where you standing here? (*Referring to
the spot where* GIAMMARCO *is standing at the moment*)

GIAMMARCO:
I don't remember!

MIMMO:
Ah, you don't remember! Let's see if Rosalia remembers it: Rosalia, your brother-in-law, before the soccer game, was he standing here?

ROSALIA:
'Nzuú!¹²

MIMMO:
'Nzuú! Did you hear Rosalia? And where was he standing?

ROSALIA (*She points to the place that is currently occupied by* GRANDMA CITTA.):
In grandma's place!

MIMMO:
In grandma's place, right! And where was grandma?

ROSALIA:
In your place!

MIMMO:
In my place! There! Now everything adds up: Giammarco, you put yourself in my spot and Grandma Citta took yours. That's why you've got my pastry now, because I, before, had put it on the floor near my slippers.

GIAMMARCO:
Should we change places, Mimmuzzo?

MIMMO:
Se.

GIAMMARCO:
It was that crazy ball's fault! When I ran after Uncle Toni's ball I swerved off and got lost on the way, Mimmuzzo!

MIMMO:
See, you got it! Now, to get back on the right path, you have to shift down this way and Grandma Citta has to shift that way. (*To* GRANDMA CITTA, *who is slow to move*) Grandma Citta, let's go, move!

GIAMMARCO, MIMMO, *and* GRANDMA CITTA *go back to their initial positions.*

GIAMMARCO:
Yes, now I remember: I was between Grandma Citta and Aunt Lucia.

MIMMO:
See you're smart after all!

GIAMMARCO:
There! Finally the pastries mix-up is resolved, can we go out? Come on, Rosalia, show us the way!

MIMMO:
Nooo! What show us the way? Stop Rosa, 'cause your brother-in-law still acts like he knows nothing! We can't go out, Giammarco, because, first, you must give me my pastry!

GIAMMARCO:
What, are you accusing me of jacking your pastry?

ROSALIA:
I've got an idea: let's do this!

MIMMO and GIAMMARCO:
What?

ROSALIA:
Let's put all the pastries on the floor again!

MIMMO:
Right! Now, I'll give a demonstration!

They all put their pastries on the ground.

MIMMO (*to GIAMMARCO*):
Let's recap: what did I say before?

GIAMMARCO:
Should we go out?

MIMMO:
And what did you answer?

GIAMMARCO:
Let's go out!

MIMMO:
And we all picked up our pastries, right?

They bend down to get their pastries.
Pause

ROSALIA (*looking sadly at the floor*):
There are no more pastries on the floor...

MIMMO:
And so?

ROSALIA:
There was no mistake, Mimmo, we all have pastries in our hands; no one's left without!

MIMMO:
What does that have to do with anything, Rosalia? Even you don't get this demonstration: I've been telling you for half an hour that this pastry isn't mine…

GRANDMA CITTA (*indicating the package in* MIMMO's *hands*):
It's mine!

Pause

MIMMO (*suddenly turning to an audience member*):
What are you looking at?

GIAMMARCO (*to* MIMMO, *indignant*):
You stole grandma's pastry! Shame on you!

MIMMO:
What? I stole the pas… I didn't steal pastries from anyone, you moron! Grandma Citta, is this pastry yours?

GRANDMA CITTA:
Yes.

MIMMO:
I took it by mistake, grandma, when, earlier, I was in your spot, you understand? Come on, take your pastry, here!

MIMMO *returns the pastry to grandma and, in exchange, he receives the packet she took from the floor when she found herself in* GIAMMARCO's *spot immediately after the soccer game. Now* MIMMO *has* GIAMMARCO's *packet in his hands and he doesn't know what's inside it. None of them know what's in the packets belonging to the others, also because the pastries are wrapped in the same kind of paper and they are all tied with the same ribbon.*

GIAMMARCO (*to* MIMMO):
There! Now you've got your blessed pastry. We can go out, folks!

MIMMO (*a scream of desperation*):
Nooo!!! This isn't mine, do you get it or not? Grandma Citta has her pastry, Rosalia has her pastry, Aunt Lucia has her pastry...

GIAMMARCO:
...Giammarco has his pastry...

MIMMO:
Giammarco doesn't have his pastry! (*Exhausted*) He's making my skull explode and blood is rising up to my cerebellum!
We have to try a different approach with him, because he's too idiotic.
(*In the calm voice one uses to talk to mad people*) Giammarco, pay attention, talk to me: the pastry you're holding tight in your fist is yours, right?

GIAMMARCO:
Se.

MIMMO:
Then, satisfy my curiosity: what's inside there?

Pause

GIAMMARCO (*gambling on the answer*):
A profiterole!

Pause

MIMMO (*taken aback*):
And satisfy me another one: what flavor is this profiterole?

Pause

GIAMMARCO (*gambling on the answer*):
Coffee!

MIMMO:
What?

Pause

GIAMMARCO:
Coffee!

MIMMO:
Coffee! (*He laughs, satisfied.*) Unwrap the pastry and show me what's inside there!

GIAMMARCO *starts to unwrap the package.*

MIMMO:
Wait! Are you in a hurry? Say it again: what flavor is this profiterole?

GIAMMARCO:
Coffee!

MIMMO:
Coffee! (*Extremely serious*) Giammarco, pay attention: as soon as this profiterole turns out to not be coffee-flavored, I'll unscrew your head, put it under my feet, and dance on top of it. Understood? (*Pause*) Open it!

GIAMMARCO *opens the packet: inside there's a chocolate profiterole.*

MIMMO (*satisfied*):
Show it to everyone!

GIAMMARCO *shows the profiterole to everyone.*

MIMMO:
So, what flavor is this profiterole?

GIAMMARCO:
Coffee!

MIMMO:
And why is it so dark?

GIAMMARCO:
Because there's chocolate mousse on the outside and, inside, there's coffee!

MIMMO:

Then, since you insist, let's do something else: take a ball of profiterole, put it in your mouth and tell us all what flavor it is!

GIAMMARCO *takes a ball of profiterole and contently chews on it.*

MIMMO:

What flavor is it?

GIAMMARCO:

Coffee!

The Little Binge

MIMMO *has been trumped and takes it in as if the roof of the house had fallen on his head. He doesn't react. Stupefied, he watches as* GIAMMARCO *destroys his profiterole and one by one swallows a ball after the other. The bastard feeds, eying his relatives, while chocolate dribbles from his mouth like the slobber of a dog gnawing on a bone.* ROSALIA *livens up and, tiptoeing on her slippers, unwraps her package and begins to peck at a little "cassata" pastry covered in icing;* AUNT LUCIA *undresses a sfinge of Saint Joseph;* GRANDMA CITTA *licks a cannoli;* MIMMO *apathetically unties the bow and unwraps a squashed croissant without any filling. Ashamed, he's about to hide that misery in his mouth when* GIAMMARCO *tears the croissant from his hands and quickly snatches all the other pastries. He amasses them, mixes them, squashes them into a single soggy mass and gets ready to devour them: he loosens his tie, stretches his legs, throws his butt out to not dirty his suit and dives face first into the amalgam of custard ricotta cinnamon chocolate hard crust candied fruits. Then he throws up and cries.*

GIAMMARCO:
I'm thirsty!

In a corner, stands a big plastic water container. Everyone looks at it with a sense of guilt, almost as if they feared damaging it with their eyes.

GIAMMARCO:
I'm thirsty!

46

Pause

ROSALIA:
Today isn't a water day![13]

GIAMMARCO:
But tomorrow is!

GRANDMA CITTA:
I'm thirsty too!

AUNT LUCIA:
Me too!

ROSALIA:
Let's drink!

MIMMO *unscrews the cap of the container, fills it with water, and gives it to his relatives.*

MIMMO (*a concession and a plea*):
Just one cap!

The Water Miracle

In religious silence, GRANDMA CITTA, ROSALIA, GIAMMARCO, *and* AUNT LUCIA *get in a line and, without wasting even a drop, they drink that little bit of water that* MIMMO *gives them. It seems blessed by the Holy Ghost. It's sacred and rare because there's a drought. But they are thirsty, poor creatures:* GRANDMA CITTA *stretches her back,* ROSALIA *takes off her slippers,* GIAMMARCO *undoes his tie and* MIMMO, *overexcited and rebellious, in the blink of an eye tosses the cap aside and sprays water everywhere as if it were champagne.*

It's a celebration. They don't give a damn about their squandering and they joke around: the women splash water under their skirts and the men spit it in each other's face. From the container spouts a waterfall that pours on a heap of drunken bodies. The water comes out in spurts. It gushes out. It penetrates the pores of their skin, it caresses them and it slaps them, it undresses them and it plunges them into the sea. They are naked and worn out. Without any more deadweight, the relieved relatives float on waves. Our gaze desecrates their naked bodies but AUNT LUCIA *is not ashamed as she advances toward us with drenched skin and bones.*

Lucia of the Sun

AUNT LUCIA:
Sono pronta!
Usciamo.
Rosalia? La mamma è pronta! Sbrigati!
Mimmo? Mi?
Let's go, I'm ready! Mi senti?
Giammarco, prendi Grandma Citta che la portiamo al mare.[14]
(*Dying with laughter*) Jee Mimmo, I said it in Italian!
Let's go out in Italian!
The sun's outside! Don't you see how beautiful this sun is?
It's big, the sun! It's yellow!
Let's go! Rosalia come here immediately!
Let's go, I'll even put on some lipstick, red!

MIMMO wrings out his wet undershirt and puts it on.

Like this, Mimmo, all wet, yes, what the fuck do we care if they're looking at us, let them look, we're going out as we are, all wet!

ROSALIA puts her slippers back on.

The wind outside will dry us up anyway! Jee... wind! Mimmo you hear me? Jee... wind!

AUNT LUCIA *gets dressed quickly and urges the others to do the same.*

Let's go, be quick, that the sun's setting! It's waiting for us. You hear me?
(*To the audience*) And you, don't go away - we're coming.
(*To the relatives*) Open the doors, open the windows, open everything
up - we've got to go out, now! Not tomorrow! Tomorrow is late. We can't
miss this train. We have to go out now, because I can't stand being in here
anymore...
We've got to leave this harbor full of stone ships. The sun's out! Don't you
see how beautiful this sun is?
(*To the audience*) The Carollo family is coming!!! Dancing dancing: the
mambo mambo!

*This time the Carollos are determined to cross the border and, pleased by
the frenetic coming and going, they jump on puddles as they pick up their
drenched rags and quickly get dressed.*

MIMMO:
Aunt Lucia, where are we going?

AUNT LUCIA:
Mimmo, don't you see how beautiful this sun is?

MIMMO (*to the audience*):
This is my aunt and I love her with all my heart!

AUNT LUCIA:
Because I'm not mute.
I can speak, I can speak in Italian. Listen, Giammarco: usciamo?[15]

GIAMMARCO:
Right, Aunt Lucia. You are the best!

AUNT LUCIA:
Run Rosalia, and I'll buy you a pair of red heels!
And for Giammarco we'll buy a mountain of pastries with whipped cream, with chocolate with ricotta…

GIAMMARCO:
The sea, Aunt Lucia! It's blue, the sea! Buy me the sea - I want to eat it!

AUNT LUCIA:
We'll bring Grandma Citta to the beach. And we'll buy her a big lifesaver, because she doesn't know how to swim!
Let's go, that I'll even put on lipstick!
You hear me?

MIMMO:
I love you with all my heart!

AUNT LUCIA:
I'm leaving! Hurry up that I'm leaving!
Open the doors, open the windows.
We have to get out now, not tomorrow!
I can't stand being in here anymore.
The sun's outside! It's yellow, the sun!
We can't miss this train!
Let's go!
Giammarco?
Get Grandma Citta!
We have to buy the lifesaver.
The sea is big! It's blue!
We have to get water!
Did we run out of water, Mimmo?
We have to buy pastries for Giammarco and red heels for Rosalia. We've run out of everything.
Let's go, hurry up…
Usciamo. Let's go out in Italian!

AUNT LUCIA, ROSALIA, GIAMMARCO and MIMMO, lined up and drenched, are ready to go out. The only one missing is GRANDMA CITTA. She remained upstage, half dressed and unable to move forward. She is tiny, grandma, a luminous dot in the middle of the sea.

MIMMO:
Grandma Citta, it's you we're waiting for. Hurry up a little, let's go!

Suddenly, grandma doubles over in pain and contorts her mouth without making a sound. The others, frightened, run toward her.

The Big Sleep

VOICES:

What's the matter, Grandma Citta?

What happened?

But why is she acting like this?

Hey, are we opening up this window?

She's gasping for air, Mimmo!

Let's go, Grandma Citta, that we've got to go out!

Call her, Aunt Lucia!

Hey, don't you see it got dark?

Grandma Citta!

Hey, can't you hear me?

It hurts!

We've got to go out, grandma, hurry up that's gotten dark!

Father, Son, and Holy Ghost, it got dark!

Fan her, Giammarco!

Hey, should I fan her with my shirt, or not?

She can't breathe…

Mimmo?

Chi duluri!

Outside there aaaaaare really amazing things, Grandma Citta!

Fan her so she can breathe!

Grandma Citta!

Call her, Aunt Lucia?

Grandma Citta!

Father, son, and the holy spirit, it got dark…

Grandma Citta?!

Grandma Citta?!

GRANDMA CITTA *dies standing up. She hunches over while breathing her last breath, but she does not fall. Hers is a death in dialect. Absurd and vulgar. The four survivors, swerving, come toward us. The sun has now set and the threshold where they stand unperturbed is the proscenium of the theatre holding them prisoners. They open their mouths wide, but their scream is a silent one. Or, rather, a yawn.*

The Butchery

◆

"When your dog has served you for many years and must die; when you want to get rid of him or he has sinned; when his skin is covered in scabs and minute animals, his ears are frazzled and bleeding, his nose is always dry and he drags his hind legs, limply hanging to one side, like dead things; or when the sight of him has become unbearable to you, do not entrust this dog who was your friend to the hands of a stranger, not even to the hands of your brother; he does not know him as you do; don't let him sense that he is dying, don't deprive him of this last token of respect: you yourself must be the one who puts him to death. Call him to a corner of the garden, give him the last bone to gnaw, caress his head with one hand and with the other, without his noticing..."[16]

— TOMMASO LANDOLFI
from "The Two Old Maids"
in *Gogol's Wife & Other Stories*

In people's faces, I've seen lizard eyes half-hidden by eyelids; horse eyes veined with blood; and cow eyes, bright and wet, filled with an inner heartbreaking tenderness.

They were humans ripped from themselves, slaughtered by an inane life. Frightened and dangerous animals that, together with their profound ability to partake in suffering, were slowly losing their kinship to humanity.

The Butchery tells the story of one of these families of meat for slaughter, with its morbid ties, its hysteric and paralyzing flights, its stagnant air smelling of smoke.

The atmosphere is festive, seemingly joyous, it is a ceremony staged to absolve a woman from sin: to clean a stain; to fix the damage; to take away dishonor from her bastard child. Nina is pregnant. Her heart is lost inside an enormous body deformed by pain and sin. Nina bears the mark. She is infected, branded. Her swollen belly is the epicenter around which her destiny unfolds; against which her three brothers, unable to understand, unleash the rage of losers. Their existence lies in their appearance. Sex, the body, territory, and property are the only motives that generate, through terrible bestiality, their full nature of fangs and claws. How to turn toward their world of beasts? How to get inside the head of a dog without catching rabies? How to get inside a pig and see things in the mud the way it sees them? Three brothers and one sister wait for the rite to take place; to wipe away an unbearable stench of filth. The wedding is ready: the priest, the church, the guests, the refreshments, the band, the flowers, the son of a bitch...

— EMMA DANTE

The Butchery premiered in November 2002 at the Teatro dell'Arte in Milan. It was produced by the CRT Centro di Ricerca per il Teatro. The production won the 2003 UBU Award. The play was written for and performed by Manuela Lo Sicco (Nina), Gaetano Bruno (Paride), Sabino Civilleri (Toruccio), and Vincenzo Di Michele (Ignazio).

CHARACTERS:

NINA

PARIDE
The eldest brother

TORUCCIO
The middle brother

IGNAZIO
The youngest brother

An altar in the dark. As in a religious procession, TORUCCIO *and* IGNAZIO *enter the space carrying* NINA *on their shoulders.* PARIDE *follows.* NINA *is wearing a wedding dress. A sash with a black cross wraps around her pregnant belly. Her hands clasp a bouquet of white daisies. She seems dead.*
Walking in religious silence, PARIDE *holds her veil outstretched and lights the way with a torch.* NINA*'s corpse is lowered to the ground. Her upright, hardened body looks like a mannequin made of meat. The three priests adorn the altar framed within the votive shrine. They wear heavy fur coats and coppolas – Sicilian flat caps. They move in jerks like animals in a cage. Cautiously, the brothers decorate the sacred place with luminarie[17] while the bride slowly slumps to the ground. She collapses three times and each time one of her brothers lifts her back up. Underneath a white cross hanging in mid-air and a canopy of tiny shining lights framing the entire scene, the curious eyes of the wedding guests sitting in the audience begin to catch details that slowly emerge from the dark: a beautiful floral arrangement in the background; a strip of cemetery candles delineating the proscenium line; and, on one side, mid-stage, a throne-like chair surmounted by a suspended half-crown made of ntertwined flower and lights. After her enchanted awakening worthy of the tales from* One Thousand and One Nights, NINA *the idiot, a fragile and helpless child, will sit on this throne whose lavishness befits an arrogant Sicilian matron. The altar is ready, the ceremony begins, and the three brothers take off their hats as a sign of respect.*

PARIDE (*speaking loudly and cheerfully to* NINA):
Wake up, Nina, we're here!

NINA *opens her eyes and lets out a big yawn, then she looks around in amazement.*

NINA:
Ooooh!

PARIDE:
You like it?

NINA:
Ooooh!

TORUCCIO:
See how pretty?

PARIDE:
Sit!

IGNAZIO:
Look what we've hung over the chair!

TORUCCIO:
Fresh flowers, Ninuzza,[18] freshly picked!

NINA (*sniffing the flowers in the air*):
Jeee!!!

TORUCCIO:
So you can rest smelling nice.

PARIDE:
Aren't you tired?

TORUCCIO:
Take a seat – we're here!

PARIDE:
Nina, did you hear Toruccio?

Pause

Sit down, *nicuzza mia*,[19] - we're finally here!

NINA:
Is it here, the meeting?

Fascinated by the audience, she dashes toward the proscenium.

PARIDE (*He halts her, pulling her by the veil.*):
Where are you going? Sit down!

NINA *responds to the command and sits.*

NINA (*referring to the spectators-intruders*):
Are they all here for me?

The brothers exchange glances without replying.
Pause
With a smile on their lips, the three brothers put their hats back on.

PARIDE:
We're coming right back!

The three start to leave but NINA follows them.

PARIDE (*to NINA*):
Where are you going?

NINA:
I'm coming with you!

PARIDE:
You can't come with us. You have to sit here! Rest. What, aren't you tired?

The three are about to go, but NINA follows them.

TORUCCIO:
What if your husband comes and doesn't find anyone, what would we do, huh? You have to tell him we're coming right back!

IGNAZIO:
Wait here like a good girl!

The three are about to run away, but NINA follows them.

TORUCCIO:
Careful! You're stepping on the veil! What, you want him to find you with the veil all wrinkled? No, right? Come on, sit down!

TORUCCIO wraps the bride in her veil like a sausage and throws her on the chair. NINA is suffocating inside the tulle casing, she pushes, she wants to get out. She violently hits her knees with her bouquet of white daisies, which suddenly lose all their petals. The petals fall to her feet and NINA frees herself from the white net.

66

NINA (*whining*):
I want to go home!

The three brothers look at the audience and feel them returning their gaze.
They exchange knowing looks. PARIDE *mutters something in* TORUCCIO's
ear. TORUCCIO *whispers something in* NINA's *ear.*

NINA (*to* TORUCCIO):
I don't care! I don't want to stay here, period!

TORUCCIO:
What do you mean you don't want to stay here! We've done so much to
make you happy: look at all these people! Look at all the lights! We had
to hook up the place with high voltage current. It cost us a fortune. What,
are we going to waste all this electricity and show nothing to your guests?
They're all here for you, do you get it or not that we're only waiting for
him to begin? And then: the flowers, the guests, the ceremony, the wedding cake, the fireworks, the honeymoon... Be a good girl, Nina, don't
make us look bad!

NINA:
I want to go back home! I don't want to stay here. I don't like this place.
Why didn't we meet him at the village? There are sheep, there, and
strawberries, and clean air, and mountains... Where did you bring me?
(*Indicating the spectators-intruders*) Who are these people? Why are they
looking at me? What do they want? (*Hysterically*) Take me back home!!!

NINA *hits* TORUCCIO *on the head with her bouquet. Rabid, he moves away*
and reciprocates his younger brother's complicit glance that invites him to keep
calm. He whispers something in PARIDE's *ear.*
The three plot animatedly. Without letting NINA *or the audience understand*
their designs, they improvise a little piece of theatre to amuse her. PARIDE

snatches the hats from his brother's heads and, together with his own, he begins to juggle them. Initially, NINA *laughs, following the three twirling hats with her eyes, but after a while the game tires her and she starts whining again. Their second act consists of organizing another escape attempt: an imaginary motorcycle ride. From his pocket,* TORUCCIO *takes out a kazoo – NINA's favorite instrument. He blows into it, imitating the sound of a motorcycle engine starting.* NINA *chuckles, and when the brothers mount the motorcycle, ready to speed away, idiotically, she also straddles the seat of an invisible motorcycle and, pleased, follows them. The engines shut off and the three brothers, exhausted, wipe away their sweat.*
NINA *inches closer to the audience, curiously observing the people sitting in front of her. They are so different from her brothers, these guests. She is ecstatic. She'd like to talk to them, to touch them...*

NINA:
Is the meeting here for sure?

She looks around and for a moment she turns her back to everyone, hopping upstage. She raises her eyes toward the ceiling and inhales deeply the smell of the flowers.

NINA:
What beautiful colored lights! What beautiful sweet-smelling flowers you brought me! Are they all here for me?

She turns to talk to the guests and notices that her brothers are about to sneak away.

NINA (*to her brothers*):
Well, why don't you take off your coats? It's hot! Sweet Lord, how hot it is! It may be better if I take this synthetic thing off my head... (*She takes*

off her wedding veil.) They make them all plasticky these wedding veils. While we wait for him, we can make ourselves comfortable, right? Paride, Toruccio… take off your coats and put them here on the chair. Oh! This chair is all dusty. Wait, I'll dust it off, so your furs won't get dirty, there!
(*She sings.*) "Amore, amore, amore… io non ho niente al mondo altro che mille ore da dedicare a te…"[20]

Resigned to their plight, the brothers take off their coats. NINA *sings while she dusts the chair with her wedding veil. She then plucks up her courage and runs to the edge of the proscenium line to speak directly to her guests.*

NINA:
We're from Roccapalumba, near Palermo.

She takes a photograph out of a hidden pocket sewn inside the sash that wraps around her waist and protects her nine months pregnant belly.

NINA (*indicating the photograph*):
This is our home, perched on this chunk of mountain! The village is near-by; (*still pointing at the picture*) it's this dot you see behind the house… In winter, the air is cool, bubbly and when it's really really cold we light the wood stove. It's Spring in this picture and everything is glowing. We went on a long journey to come all the way here and I don't really know how to go back the way we came. We took the ferry. The ferry went through the Messina Strait and I waved to the little Madonna of the pier as she became smaller and smaller while we moved away. From the ferry I saw fish swimming and breathing in the water. But how can they breathe in water? He he he! Who knows? And there were seagulls too! Jeee… how many seagulls! They flew above the sea and above our heads and they cried and cried…

What did they sound like, Paride? (*PARIDE imitates the seagulls and NINA laughs.*) He he he! My brothers arranged this wedding! They take care of me! It's true!
She starts taking out the stack of photographs she keeps inside the sash.

NINA:
My mama, on the day of her wedding! This dress I'm wearing was my mama's. But the thing is, when I put it on the zipper didn't close because I keep getting fatter. He he he! Maybe it's the pasta! I myself like pasta with tomato sauce. When I make it, Paride cleans his plate and then licks it too. He he he! What a pig!!! (*Another picture*) Grandma Carmela! Jeee… how mean she was! If you'd take something from the pantry: bam! She'd whack your fingers. She'd lock up candies, shortbread cookies, chocolate… (*Another picture*) Our grandparents at the produce market: they had a fruits and vegetables stand in Palermo. (*Another picture*) Mama and papa dancing! (*She thinks about it.*) They're all dead.
That's why I brought them with me. So we're all here!

NINA attempts something like a dance step while she cradles the photos she's just taken out of her pregnant belly.

NINA (*another picture*):
Paride, when he was little. Wasn't he cute? Here he's wearing his school uniform. The sleeves are too short for him, because Paride's arms are too long. Dressing him has always been a problem because blazers, coats, fur coats… they all made him look like a scarecrow! He he he!

PARIDE:
What are you saying, Nina?

NINA:
Don't get mad, Paride dear! I'm joking! Look how cute you were holding your favorite book under your arm. (*To the audience*) He liked math, he

always studied it! (*Solemnly*) Paride knows everything! Ask him anything, he knows it. Paride, how much is four times four?

PARIDE:
Forty-four?

The brothers laugh.

NINA (*another picture*):
Ignazio and Toruccio holding hands: Ignazio is the smallest one, next to the Christmas tree. Toruccio was missing his front teeth and since he was ashamed, he held a hand in front of his mouth when he laughed!

The brothers come closer. They are curious. NINA, *excited, shows them the pictures.*

PARIDE:
Where did you get these pictures, Nina? We haven't seen them in years.

TORUCCIO:
Centuries, Paride!

NINA:
There's so many of them.

PARIDE:
And why aren't you showing us all of them?

PARIDE, TORUCCIO, *and* IGNAZIO *take possession of the pictures, grabbing them from their sister's hands.*

NINA:

I wasn't there in these pictures. I wasn't born yet. But I've become attached to them because, even if I wasn't there, my mama and my papa were...

PARIDE:

Good girl, Ninuzza, you brought them all! Even the ones from that Carnival party... (*To TORUCCIO*) Talè ccà![21]

TORUCCIO:

It's me, dressed up like Pierrot. I won a trophy. You remember, Paride?

PARIDE:

Se,[22] a big one! (*Mocking him*) A big, hard one you won!!!

IGNAZIO:

Look: it's grandpa, bless his soul! He always wore his hair pulled back with Linetti pomade, do you remember?

PARIDE:

Grandpa Paride! I'm his namesake.

TORUCCIO:

Look what I found, Paride! Our cousins from Germany. What were their names?

PARIDE:

Hans, Raus and the other one, what was his name Ignazio?

IGNAZIO:

Ugo Von de Bruggenstein.

Pause
The brothers look at each other and almost die laughing.

TORUCCIO and PARIDE:
Ugo Von de Bruggenstein.

PARIDE:
Right: with the long last name! Good memory Ignazieddu:[23] "The group's historian!"

IGNAZIO:
Paride, look, aunt Nunù, your favorite!

TORUCCIO:
The looney!

PARIDE (*speaking directly to the guests*):
My aunt Nunù had very confused ideas about life, except for one thing: breakfast. She always said that when it comes to eating, everything can be incoherent, except for breakfast, which has to be rich, nutritious, and abundant. In fact, I remember that every morning at six thirty sharp, because she was punctual my aunt, truth be told...

TORUCCIO:
A Swiss clock!

PARIDE:
...at six thirty, she would round us all up and she'd bring us to the chicken shed. She'd line us up and gather freshly laid eggs. She'd put an egg in our left hand, a toothpick in the right, tap tap tap: a tiny crack and a big suck! Every morning at six thirty... I hated my aunt!

TORUCCIO:
Don't get mad, Paride, the crazy bat's dead!

IGNAZIO:
Look: mom and dad on their wedding day, when they had their picture taken under the Garibaldi statue.

NINA:
How beautiful mom was! Do I look like her, Paride? Am I as pretty as her?

PARIDE:
You're prettier!

NINA:
Se! But you always tell me I look like a monkey!

PARIDE:
And who said monkeys are ugly?

PARIDE pats her cheek.
TORUCCIO laughs uncontrollably as he waves around a photo that PARIDE and IGNAZIO cannot clearly see.

PARIDE (*trying to keep the picture in TORUCCIO's hands from moving*):
Hold it steady! If you don't, I can't look at it, you idiot! Stop moving it, I said! (*He rips it from his hands and studies it.*) And who's this?

TORUCCIO:
What you mean "who's this"? You don't recognize him? Ignazio, dressed like a girl!! With a little pink dress and a bow in his hair! Get that picture away from me, Paride, I can't look at it, it's obscene!

TORUCCIO continues to laugh. PARIDE looks more carefully at the photo.

PARIDE:
You're wrong, Toruccio. That's your cousin Graziella on the rocking horse!

TORUCCIO:
It's Ignazio!

PARIDE:
It's Graziella!

IGNAZIO snatches the picture from PARIDE's hands and, after examining it, sneers with satisfaction. His laughter sounds like a combustion engine. Everyone stares at him, shocked.

TORUCCIO:
What's happening to him?

PARIDE:
He's warming up the chopper!

TORUCCIO:
He's about to take off...

PARIDE:
Talè...

TORUCCIO:
He's gaining altitude!

PARIDE:
Now that the engine's going, Ignazio, let us come on board too: what do you see from up there?

IGNAZIO (*showing the photograph to the audience*):
It's Toruccio!

No one laughs anymore except for IGNAZIO *who continues to wave the picture in the faces of the audience.*

PARIDE:
You keep us hanging, Ignazio, making us believe that you know God knows what truth, and half an hour later you spit out this stratospheric pile of shit? (*He tears the picture from his hands and shows it to* NINA. *Threatening*) Nina, who's this?

NINA:
Ignazio?

TORUCCIO (*feeling relieved, cheerfully*):
You see, it's Ignazio!

PARIDE:
Wrap it up, don't you know your sister is half stupid?

TORUCCIO:
Idiots always speak the truth, Paride!

PARIDE:
I'm telling you it's Graziella!

IGNAZIO (*He retakes the photo from* PARIDE, *turns to the audience, and speaks with conviction.*):
This here is Toruccio, dressed like a girl, with a little pink dress and a little bow!

PARIDE:
So you really didn't get it that you've got to drop it?!

IGNAZIO:
Now I can drop it!

PARIDE:
And put that photo away!

IGNAZIO:
I'm putting it away.

IGNAZIO hides the photo behind his back.

PARIDE:
When we get home, you've just got to burn it. Do you understand me,
you moron?

IGNAZIO:
Sure, I understand Paride. Do you think I'm deaf like middle brother
there? As soon as we get home, I'll burn this fucking picture and we're not
going to talk about it anymore, all right?

TORUCCIO:
No! What do you mean we're not going to talk about it anymore? You
can't just get out of it like this, Ignazieddu! Paride, I'm sorry, would you
hold these photos of our lovely family for me since they've all ended up in
my hands for no reason? (*He gives the pictures to PARIDE.*) Thank you.
Ignazio! You've already gotten to the prologue and I haven't even given
you an introduction! Relax! First, I'll speak and then, after I'm done, you
can wrap it up with a nice postlude, huh?

IGNAZIO:
And who taught you that word?

TORUCCIO:
I read it in a textbook. It seems he thinks I'm ignorant, Paride!

PARIDE:

How could that be, Toruccio? We all drank from the same fountain! Textbooks are all the same, we can't really forget them…

TORUCCIO:

Right? Mom smacked our backs with a wooden spoon to make us study.

NINA:

Jee, how many spoons did mommy break on your back, Paride? He he he!!!

PARIDE:

Shut up, you! Amunì,[24] Toruccio. Just make peace with your brother and let's not talk about it anymore!

TORUCCIO:

Uh-uh! I've promised him an introduction and I can't refuse now! After all, he's still my brother even if he's been insulting me for the past half hour, right?

PARIDE:

Amunì, Toruccio, drop it! What the fuck do you care? Let him stew in his own juice!

TORUCCIO:

I'm not ignorant, Ignazio, and I'm not deaf either, not from the right nor from the left, because, it's not like, all of a sudden, I got struck by a lightening ear infection and I suddenly turned deaf right and left, isn't that right Paride? And, as far as I can historically remember, I don't recall there being in the genealogical tree of the Cuore family any ill-timed episodes of Parkinson's disease, and, if I am shaking right now it's just to show you that my hand is usually steady as a leaf waiting for fall. All these things said and wrapped up in bows for Easter, Saint Joseph, and all the damned Saints, 'gnazio, you, who don't know how to read and write, you told me that I'm wearing a little pink dress, a bow in my hair, and that I am dressed like a girl. Therefore, logic would have it that you called me a "fag"!

Pause

IGNAZIO:
No. I didn't say you're a fag, Toruccio!

Pause

TORUCCIO:
No, huh?

IGNAZIO:
No.

PARIDE:
He didn't call you a fag, Toruccio!

Pause

TORUCCIO:
Ignazio, give me that picture and let's show everyone who's in it, amunì!

IGNAZIO holds the photo out to him but doesn't allow TORUCCIO to take it.

PARIDE (*to TORUCCIO*):
But, if he gives it to you, you have to take it, right?

*PARIDE tries to break the ice and to get TORUCCIO involved in
IGNAZIO's game. They joke around but the atmosphere is charged.*

TORUCCIO:
Ignazio I don't like this game, stop it, you're getting on my nerves!

PARIDE:
Why are you getting mad, Toruccio? We're just messing around!

TORUCCIO:
I said: give me that photo, Ignazio!

PARIDE:
Amunì, 'gnazieddu, give him the photo, otherwise he's going to cry!

IGNAZIO:
I want to give it to him, but he doesn't want it. Otherwise he'd have
already taken it, right? It means he doesn't deserve it.

NINA (*to IGNAZIO*):
Put it between his legs, Ignazio! Go on Toruccio, bend down to get it…
He he he!

*NINA laughs and jokes around without understanding the gravity of the
situation.*

TORUCCIO:
This game won't end well, Ignazio! I keep it inside, keep it inside…

IGNAZIO:
There, you almost had it. Jee, you're so easily distracted!

PARIDE:

You're not paying attention, Toruccio! Amuní, relax! Don't think about it. Give me a pretty smile!

PARIDE pinches TORUCCIO's cheek.

TORUCCIO (*aggressively*):

Take your hands off my face!

Pause
The brothers suddenly become very serious. PARIDE reproachingly stares at TORUCCIO first and then at IGNAZIO. You could hear a pin drop. IGNAZIO takes courage and, clicking his tongue, makes a strange noise with his mouth. It is like a slap directed at TORUCCIO.

IGNAZIO:

Clip-clop clip-clop clip-clop! "Toruccio let's play horsey!"

PARIDE:

Ignazio, stop it. Are you crazy?

IGNAZIO:

"Toruccio let's play horsey!"

PARIDE:

Stop it Ignazio!

NINA:

"Let's play horsey," clip-clop clip-clop clip-clop...

PARIDE:
Ignazio, make your sister stop!

IGNAZIO:
Clip-clop clip-clop clip-clop

PARIDE *brutally slaps* IGNAZIO *in the head and* IGNAZIO's *hat flies off.*

PARIDE (*to* IGNAZIO, *threatening*):
Get your hat!

IGNAZIO *puts the hat back on. Using his mouth he once again makes the sound of a horse trotting and directs it at* TORUCCIO. NINA *mechanically repeats the same sound.* PARIDE *slaps* IGNAZIO *multiple times and covers* NINA's *mouth, but it is too late. Everyone slowly enters* TORUCCIO's *memories, reliving the abuses and injustices of their childhood.* PARIDE *and* IGNAZIO *dance.* NINA *sits down and, after uncovering one of her breasts, she breastfeeds her still unborn child.* TORUCCIO *stands downstage alone. He too clicks his tongue, suggesting the trot of his little horse.*
A time-shift chills the atmosphere. The first secret of the Cuore family emerges from an auditory tangle of voices and noises evoking the childhood home where the four young siblings lived with their parents.

NINA:
"Toruccio, let's play horsey!" Toruccio! Toruccio!

IGNAZIO:
"Come! *Come!*"

PARIDE (*imitating their father's voice*):
"Toruccio?"

TORUCCIO:
My name is Salvatore![25]

PARIDE:
"Come to me!"

IGNAZIO:
Where's dad?

TORUCCIO:
I really loved my dad! He'd always tell me: Toruccio, in my house you are the man!

NINA:
"We are both men!"

TORUCCIO:
"Men have beards."

IGNAZIO and **PARIDE:**
"Toruccio, dressed like a girl!"

TORUCCIO (*imitating his father's voice*):
"Toruccio, put on your mother's shoes!"

IGNAZIO:
Walk my little dancer!

TORUCCIO (*uncovering his legs*):
They're skinny, dad!

NINA:
Beautiful, beautiful, beautiful, you're so beautiful!

IGNAZIO and **PARIDE:**
"Fags are beautiful!"

TORUCCIO:
Like Jesus who's no longer with us!

PARIDE (*imitating his father's voice*):
"Dad loves you with all his heart."

NINA:
Toruccio, vistùto 'i fimmina![26]

PARIDE:
My God, I am heartily sorry for having offended you, and I detest all my sins, because of your just punishments, but most of all, because they offend you, my God, who are all good and deserving of all my love...

TORUCCIO (*imitating his father's voice*):
"Give me your hands. I'll warm them up for you!"

ALL:
Want to see what happens if you don't quit crying?

TORUCCIO *puts one hand behind his back and begins to move it. He's masturbating his father who is standing behind him.*

TORUCCIO:
Jeee dad!!! It sticks out and goes back in! (*Imitating his father's voice*) "Shut up!"

ALL:
Boom!!! The door!

TORUCCIO:
It sticks out and goes back in, daddy!

NINA:
"Let me in!"

PARIDE:
Go away, Nina!

IGNAZIO:
Paride, close the windows!

PARIDE:
Where is dad?

NINA:
Mommy went out.

IGNAZIO:
Come here, come here…

NINA:
"Beautiful, beautiful, beautiful, you're so beautiful!"

IGNAZIO and PARIDE:
"Fags are beautiful!"

NINA:
Like Jesus who's no longer with us!

PARIDE (*imitating his father's voice*):
"Give me your hands. I'll warm them up for you!"

TORUCCIO (*imitating his father's voice*):
"Toruccio, let's play horsey!"

TORUCCIO *moves in jerks, a movement that is halfway between that of a trotting horse and a rape. He's in a trance.*

TORUCCIO:
"Dad loves you with all his heart!"
I get tired dad! Wait! I'm tired, daddy! Like Jesus who's no longer with us!
"Pray with me: My God, I am heartily sorry for having offended you, and
I detest all my sins, because of your just punishments…"
Wait, daddy, I'm tired!
"Want to see what happens if you don't quit crying?"
Wait dad, I'm tired!
Let me in! Boom!!! The door!
Mommy went out.
"Beautiful, beautiful, beautiful you're so beautiful! Toruccio, let's play
horsey!"
Men have beards!
It sticks out and goes back in, daddy… Boom the door!
(*Screaming*) Paride, you are next!

PARIDE *slaps* IGNAZIO *on the head and* IGNAZIO'*s hat flies off.*
TORUCCIO'*s memory suddenly dissolves. The action returns to the previous
scene, in which the brothers were talking about the identity of the person in
the photo.*

PARIDE (*to* IGNAZIO, *threatening*):
Get your hat! (*He shows* TORUCCIO *the photo he holds in his hand.*) This
is Graziella!

Pause

TORUCCIO (*pointing at* IGNAZIO):
Actually, it's that son of a cocksucker!

IGNAZIO:
You come here and say it to my face.

TORUCCIO:
Who just spoke? A fly?

IGNAZIO:
And who do you think you are? A lion from the forest surrounding this cock's dick head?

PARIDE:
I said wrap it up, Ignazio! Don't provoke him!

TORUCCIO:
And since when have flies been given the gift of speech?

IGNAZIO charges at TORUCCIO, but PARIDE gets in the middle and prevents him from reaching his brother.

IGNAZIO
You have to say it right in my ear if you have the guts because, otherwise, I don't hear you… Your voice doesn't go through my Eustachian tubes!

TORUCCIO (*imitating a fly*):
Bzzz! I hear an annoying buzzing. Paride, can you tell me who's disturbing my peace?

PARIDE:
Toruccio, drop it I said – or it will all go to shit!

IGNAZIO:
Do you get it, you damn traitor? If you don't zip your mouth shut, I'll stretch your asshole as wide as a crate and your words, I'll make them come out directly from the same place where your shit comes out…

TORUCCIO (*to* IGNAZIO):
You'll do what? You poor, useless thing?

IGNAZIO:
I'll pulverize you!

TORUCCIO:
You know what, 'gnazieddu, you can suck it! You're a nobody mixed with nothing! Don't you ever forget it: "Suck it! Suck it! Suck it"

IGNAZIO:
It wasn't enough for dad to suck it, huh?

PARIDE:
Ignazio, if you keep going, I'll butcher you!

IGNAZIO:
Why? Isn't it true, Paride? Don't we all know the truth?

PARIDE:
All I know is that if you say anything else, I'll take off my belt…

TORUCCIO:
He remembers everything, Ignazieddu: "The historian of the group." But, Paride, do you think Ignazieddu remembers when dad would measure him and he'd tell us that Ignazio's dick wouldn't get any bigger, not even when he watched porn? It's small, Ignazio, and it will stay small for the rest of your life!

IGNAZIO:
Fucking faggot!

TORUCCIO:
What did you say to me?

PARIDE:
He wasn't talking to you!

IGNAZIO:
I said you're a faggot!

TORUCCIO (*He hurls himself at* IGNAZIO, *furious.*):
What did you say to me?

Wild with rage, PARIDE *goes toward* NINA. *He tosses the pictures on the ground and threatens to hit her.*

PARIDE:
Do you fucking see what you've done? It's your fault your brothers are killing each other... if you hadn't brought those fucking pictures, everything would have gone smooth as silk... damn you!

NINA (*screaming to defend herself*):
Paride?

During the clash with TORUCCIO, IGNAZIO *loses his balance and shoves* PARIDE *who, in turn, pushes* TORUCCIO *to keep him away from* IGNAZIO. *A vicious fight breaks out between the three brothers.* NINA, *frightened, seizes the opportunity to pick up the photos and hide behind the chair.* PARIDE *immobilizes his brothers by grabbing them by the scruff of their necks like a dog with her puppies.*

PARIDE:
What are we going to do, you bastards? Are we going to kill each other like dogs over this bullshit or are we going to go through with our noble plan? Get me that picture right now and I'll show you that I was right, go!!!

TORUCCIO and IGNAZIO search for the photograph on the ground, but they can't find it. This intensifies their rage.

IGNAZIO:
It's not here, Paride, it's not here anymore!

PARIDE:
What do you mean? Look for it, it must be here!

TORUCCIO:
I can't find it, goddammit!!!

PARIDE (*now also looking for the picture*):
Where is it? Where did it go?

IGNAZIO:
It must be here!
PARIDE (*indicating the place where they are looking*):
I threw the photos over here, where the fuck are they?

Suddenly, the brothers' eyes light up and their focus shifts to NINA. She took the pictures. It's her fault. Now it's her turn. PARIDE asks his sister for the stack of pictures she holds in her lap. NINA gives it to him without raising her eyes.

PARIDE (*looking for the incriminating picture among the stack*):
Now let's look for our beloved picture, this way you'll admit, once and for all, that you were all wrong because it's not Ignazio, it's not Toruccio, but it's our bitch of a cousin Graziella! (*PARIDE finds the picture and shows it to everyone.*) Is this it?

IGNAZIO:
That's it.

PARIDE:
Nina, who's this?

NINA (*trembling*):
Ignazio?

PARIDE:
What do you mean, Ignazio! (*He laughs.*) I smashed in both their heads and you tell me it's Ignazio? Then you're completely stupid! Take a good look, Nina, concentrate. (*He stops laughing and raises his voice.*) Who is it?

NINA:
Graziella?

PARIDE:
Graziella! (*To* TORUCCIO) Who is this here?

TORUCCIO:
Graziella.

PARIDE (*to* IGNAZIO):
Who is it?

IGNAZIO:
Graziella.

PARIDE:
Oooooh! And I don't want to have to say it again, understood? Get it into your thick heads that when Paride tells you something...

PARIDE *drops the photo, pretending it slipped from his hands.*

PARIDE (*with regret*):
Talè, Graziella fell down!

Pause

PARIDE:
Nina, could you please pick Graziella up for me?

Pause
NINA raises her eyes and looks first at PARIDE and then at the other two brothers. She gets up slowly, knowing that her punishment is coming. Resigned, she bends down to get the photo. TORUCCIO, with fake clumsiness, puts a foot on the photo. The poor girl tries every possible way to free the picture stuck under her brother's shoe, but PARIDE commands her attention and asks her to collect, without standing up, the annoying pictures that fall out of his hands as if they were alive. The more NINA crawls at their feet, the more the three bastards get aroused.

PARIDE:
Thank you, Ninuzza! If you only knew how much he loves you, your Paride, when he sees you being a sensible little girl!

TORUCCIO:
Obedient...

PARIDE:
Toruccio, out of curiosity: when I tell you to do something, what do you do?

TORUCCIO:
What, wouldn't I do anything for you, Paride?

PARIDE:
And you, 'gnazieddu, do you question the why and the how, or do you just get going?

IGNAZIO:
I go off like a rocket, Paride!

PARIDE:
Isn't that right? Like when dad used to say: Paride, go buy me some cigarettes, fly! (*He makes his father's picture fly.*) Talè, dad flew away!

Pause
Without even waiting for PARIDE'*s command,* NINA *creeps toward her father's picture and, breathing heavily, lies down on her side to get few seconds of rest before she begins crawling again to collect the rest of the pictures.*

But I, little bastard, instead of cigarettes I bought myself candy. I'd go back home, lock myself in my room, and I'd eat them all. Mommy, then, would grab me by the ears and say: "This isn't right, it isn't right, it isn't right!" (*He drops his mother's photo*) Nina since you're already down there, would you pick up mommy for me as well?

IGNAZIO:
You'll wear her out like this, Paride!

TORUCCIO (*ostentatiously worried*):
You're wearing her out, Paride!

PARIDE:
You should stay at your sister's side, then! Don't move away, Toruccio, help her pick up the family photos she carried in her belly with so much love!
Ignazio, in your opinion, why do I have to repeat things two, or three times to your sister?

IGNAZIO:
Maybe she's deaf?

PARIDE:
Toruccio, do you hear well?

TORUCCIO:
I told you Paride: no ear infections yet. My ears work well, both the right and the left one.

PARIDE (*showing the photos to* TORUCCIO):
Did you give her these pictures?

TORUCCIO:
To who?

PARIDE:
To your sister.

TORUCCIO:
Me? No! I swear! (*He makes the sign of the cross.*) I swear it on the Madonna and baby Jesus!

PARIDE (*showing the photos to* IGNAZIO):
Did 'gnazieddu give them to her, then?

IGNAZIO:
Me? Absolutely not, Paride! I didn't give them to her. I'd never dream of doing something without asking you first.

PARIDE:
But then I don't understand anything anymore! (*He raps on his head.*) Because, if Ignazio didn't give them to her, and Toruccio didn't give them to her, then it means that Nina took them herself, without asking for permission! Isn't that true, Ninuzza?

Pause
NINA, on all fours, drags herself around, and, like a scared dog that knows it will be beaten very shortly, she does not dare to raise her eyes.

Aw, why do you make that sad face? Are you scared? Don't you worry, blood of mine. Look at me! Paride loves you with all his heart, and if he tells you not to do something, he says it for your own good! Come on, come here, little one, so Paride can coddle you. Don't make that sad face. Come!

NINA crawls toward PARIDE.

You have to laugh, joy of mine! You have to have fun! Soon your prince charming will come and he has to find you beaming, not with that long face… (*Speaking to TORUCCIO and IGNAZIO*) Then she says that her brothers don't love her!

TORUCCIO:
She's ungrateful!

IGNAZIO (*to NINA*):
Enjoy the most beautiful day of your life!

TORUCCIO:
Any other girl would be happy in your place!

PARIDE (*to NINA*):
Did you hear your brothers? You have to enjoy all these God-given delights! What's the point of digging up the past? The dead are dead and you have to leave them at peace. Tomorrow you start a new life! You hear me?

It looks like NINA *is no longer listening. She stares catatonically at the stack of pictures she holds in her hands. She spreads them open like a fan and, after counting them, she whiningly offers them to* PARIDE.

NINA:
Maybe it's better if you keep them with the rest!

PARIDE (*angry*):
So you don't hear me when I speak! It's true you're deaf! (*He grabs her by the hair.*) I told you not to worry about those fucking pictures anymore and to stop whining, you hear me? You've got to laugh, Nina, you've got to be happy, like when we were on the boat, remember? There were seagulls. (*He imitates a seagull with his voice.*) Do you remember the cries of the seagulls?
I hugged you and you laughed and you told me: "Paride, can you catch that seagull for me?" And I tried to catch it, Nina dear! I leaned against the deck railing and tried to grab the whole flock of seagulls flying above our heads!
(*He tosses all the photos in the air.* NINA *tries to grab the ones she can.*)
Don't you dare, ever again, do anything before asking me for permission. Open your arms?

NINA *obeys the command and, goggling her eyes, opens her arms.* PARIDE *kicks her in the belly. The violence of the impact flings* NINA *backward. She lets out a muffled scream. Then, as a sign of submission, she gives back to* PARIDE *the slim stack of photographs that was left in her hands.*

NINA:
Paride, take them back home!

Beaming, PARIDE *turns to his brothers.*

PARIDE:
Did you hear? "Take them back home" Ninuzza said. That means that we can go, right?
(*TORUCCIO and IGNAZIO do not move.*) What is it? Why are you just standing there? Move, Toruccio! What the fuck are you doing, Ignazio? Get your hat, amunì!

TORUCCIO and IGNAZIO, petrified, are looking toward the audience. PARIDE, once again, becomes aware of their presence. He had completely forgotten about them. For a moment, his legs shake. He feels watched. He's full of shame for having aired so much dirty laundry. PARIDE makes his brothers understand that they better get out of there quickly. He puts the photos in his pocket, pulls himself together, and gestures to the other two to pick up their hats and coats. Embarrassed and confused, TORUCCIO puts on PARIDE's fur coat while PARIDE takes IGNAZIO's and IGNAZIO wears TORUCCIO's. Confident that this time no-one is going to stop them, they lower their heads and, without goodbyes, move toward the exit. But a sudden movement of NINA's belly makes her jump two feet. PARIDE turns and sees NINA twisting in pain. Her belly moves, thrashing left and right as if it were possessed. With terror in their eyes the three brothers follow their sister's jumps and pirouettes. In the throes of the contractions and the tremors of her giant belly, NINA is about to give birth.

PARIDE (*shocked*):
Nina, what's happening to you?

NINA:
It's moving!

Pause

TORUCCIO:
That's normal!

NINA:
No, it's not that normal!

Pause
Her belly flings her from side to side, spreading panic everywhere. NINA *asks her brothers for help. They don't know if they should run away or improvise some sort of emergency treatment. They're afraid.*

PARIDE:
Nina, I've got an idea: why don't you take that sash off, so you can breathe better? Good girl! Let's start there: take off the sash, it's squashing you!

NINA *obeys and, actually, her belly seems to subside for a moment. Everyone breathes a sigh of relief but that's when the turmoil begins anew and* NINA *jumps and screams like a possessed creature.*

NINA:
It's still moving!

PARIDE:
Breathe, listen to me, Nina, don't think about it!

NINA:
It feels like an earthquake inside me, Paride!

PARIDE:
Calm down, fill up your chest and take long, deep breaths. Use your arm, like this! Good girl! You've got to find the right movement for you: one

and two, and one and two…Toruccio, Ignazio let's breathe with her: one and two, and one and two…

IGNAZIO:
Paride, what the fuck are you doing?

PARIDE:
Breathe, Ignazio! One and two, and one and two…

IGNAZIO:
One and two, and one and two…

PARIDE:
Toruccio, tell her something, distract her!

TORUCCIO:
Nina, listen to your brother Toruccio: you can't do it now because if your husband gets here and finds it already done, what kind of a shitty first impression would we make?

IGNAZIO and PARIDE:
Right!!!

NINA:
It moves by itself!

IGNAZIO:
How is it moving by itself? It's not possible. You're the one who's making it move!

PARIDE:
It's your sick head! It's suggestion!

TORUCCIO (*to PARIDE*):
But how many does she have in there, Paride? Sixteen?

PARIDE:
Could that ever be, Toruccio? Stop spewing that shit!

TORUCCIO (*to IGNAZIO*):
The Battleship Poteomki!!![27]

IGNAZIO (*laughing*):
Nina, how many do you want to pop out? One, right?

TORUCCIO:
One is enough, Ninuzza!

NINA *squats down, opens her legs and pushes. She pushes with all her might while she takes off her underwear.*

What the fuck are you doing? Close your legs! Stop it, Nina, otherwise I'll kill you, you understand? Your thighs have to stay shut, damn you!

NINA:
I can't do it! It's not my fault, I swear! Paride, I'm dying!

PARIDE:
You're not dying monkey, you're not dying! Hold on and I'll give you a present later!

NINA:
Make it come out, Paride! I beg you! Pull it out! I can't hold it anymore…

PARIDE:
Nooo! I said no! And when Paride says something he says it for your own good…

NINA:
I feel like I'm dying!

TORUCCIO:
Sing, Nina, don't think about it. Sing that song you like so much: "Amore, amore mio, queste mie mani vuote sono piene solamente di carezze per te…"[28]

NINA *has very strong contractions. A lacerating scream of pain makes the brothers run away from her.*

NINA (*desperate, to* PARIDE):
Nooo! Paride! Wait. Don't go. Not now, please. I'm sick. Just one more minute… Parideee! Help me, for the love of God!

PARIDE, *followed by the others, goes back to* NINA *but instead of helping her, he insults her mercilessly.*

PARIDE (*to* NINA):
You're nothing but a traitor! Stop it, you bitch! Everyone is looking at us. If you don't stop it, Paride leaves, you understand? I'll let you to die like a dog!

NINA:
It's not my fault, Paride. It moves by itself. It hurts!!!

NINA *has another contraction. She screams and slumps down.* PARIDE *uses his fur coat to cover* NINA *from the waist down and invites the others to do the same. No-one should see what will come out from inside her.*

PARIDE:
Stop it, I told you! And when Paride tells you to do something, he says it for your own good… Do you have to pop out this bastard right now?

IGNAZIO:
Now is not the time, Nina!

TORUCCIO:
What are we going to do, Paride?

PARIDE:
Shut up! Talk to her, for fuck's sake! Make her change her mind. And cover her up!

TORUCCIO:
Yeah, I'm covering her up, goddammit, but if the baby is born what the fuck are we going to do with it?

PARIDE:
I don't know, I don't know…

IGNAZIO:
It's too late! We should have gone earlier… It's all Graziella's fault, that bitch!

PARIDE:
Nina, don't do it! Don't you do it!

NINA *continues to scream and contort in pain.* PARIDE *blackmails her and makes her believe that this time he'll really leave her.*

Look, Nina, I'm putting on my fur coat and I'm going, once and for all. (*He goes to put on the fur coat and he realizes that it isn't his coat.*) This isn't my coat.

IGNAZIO:
It's mine, Paride. Maybe I have yours... Is this it?

PARIDE (*to IGNAZIO*):
Give me my coat!

PARIDE throws his fur coat to IGNAZIO who throws him the one he is holding. NINA follows the strange flutter with her eyes.

PARIDE (*to NINA*):
There, Paride is getting dressed and is going to leave! (*He goes to put on the coat and realizes that this one is not his either.*) Really? What are we playing at? This isn't my coat either. Amunì, I'm really enjoying this game! You idiots: who has my coat?

TORUCCIO:
I have it, Paride. This is yours and that's mine.

PARIDE:
So, give it to me, what are you waiting for?

TORUCCIO:
Here!

As TORUCCIO throws the coat to PARIDE and PARIDE throws him his, NINA follows their flight. She's almost amused.

TORUCCIO (*noticing her sister's reaction, stunned*):
Paride, she likes the flying furs!

PARIDE:
What are you talking about?

TORUCCIO (*to PARIDE*):
Shake the coat for her! Talè: she likes it, she's laughing! Nina? Look at
Paride!

*Shaking the fur coat like a red cloth in front of a bull, PARIDE lures NINA
center stage. She is surrounded by her brothers who make the furs fly above
her head like a flock of seagulls. The demented girl, for a moment, forgets
about her contractions and, as in a dream, transforms the pain into a merry
carousel.*

PARIDE:
Talè, Nina: they're flying! (*Paride and the others toss each other the furs to
make them fly.*) Just like seagulls! Look!

TORUCCIO:
It's working, she likes it, the little one, talè! Nina! Look how they glide!

IGNAZIO:
Toruccio, throw it! Nina, talè, they're crying out!

*IGNAZIO cries out like a seagull.
The three brothers circle around NINA. The air moved by the flying coats lifts
NINA's dress, uncovering her thighs. Aroused, the brothers encourage her to
undress.*

TORUCCIO:
Do you like it, Ninuzza?

PARIDE:
Show me your legs, my love. Dance for me, Nina, dance!

IGNAZIO:
Put on some lipstick!

PARIDE:
Beautiful, beautiful, beautiful, you're so beautiful!

TORUCCIO:
Let down your hair, life of mine!

IGNAZIO:
Come here! Come here!

TORUCCIO:
Give me your hands, I'll warm them up for you!

IGNAZIO:
Walk my little dancer!

TORUCCIO:
Ah, little whore!

PARIDE:
Toruccio, see how beautiful your sister is when she laughs?

TORUCCIO:
You are too beautiful, monkey!

NINA uncovers her legs, puts lipstick on, lets down her hair, and, to excite her men in heat, catches a flying coat and sensually puts it on. In a flash, the bride becomes a whore and bird feathers come out from her battered belly. In this chaos of furs and feathers, a stylized orgy takes place. NINA screams and the three brothers, exhausted, kneel at her feet. The spell breaks and NINA, bent over from her labor pains, slowly gets up as she clutches her three dogs.

NINA (*to her guests, while she strokes her belly*):
This baby is good! It's already the third time he's tried to come out. But I hold him back and he goes to sleep. "Now it's not the time," I tell him! "It's not the time! Uncle Paride says that we have to wait."

As she continues to stroke her belly, she sings a lullaby to the baby to help him fall asleep.

NINA:
This baby is a saint! One night I had a dream: I dreamt of big golden wings and when Paride woke me up I was all wet.

Pause

NINA:
Paride and I sleep in the same bed. In the double bed that was my parents.' Once in a while Ignazio and Toruccio come visit us. We all sleep together.

Pause

NINA (*to PARIDE*):
My husband loves me, doesn't he Paride?

PARIDE (*He stands up and moves away, ashamed.*):
He loves you.

NINA (*to TORUCCIO*):
My husband is thin, isn't he Toruccio?

TORUCCIO stands up and moves away.

(*to* IGNAZIO) And he is handsome too, because looks also matter, isn't that how the saying goes, Ignazio?

IGNAZIO moves away.

I too love him, even though I've never seen him.
Because my husband respects me!

Pause
NINA *picks up the hats and the coats from the ground, gives them to her brothers, and helps them get dressed.*

Paride, put these on, it's late! Come on, Ignazio, put on your hat, otherwise your head will freeze. Toruccio, fix your shirt: it's all wrinkled and I just ironed it this morning.
In the house where I'll go, I don't want locks on the doors and I want the windows to be always open.
I will go buy bread, that way I'll meet other girls and we'll chat, I'll make some friends, we'll get to know each other...
On Christmas Day and Easter, my husband, the baby and I will go visit you. My husband knows the way back to the village, right Paride?

PARIDE:
He knows it by heart.

Pause

NINA (*to her brothers, worried*):
What will you do without me? Poor dears! Who's going to wash your underwear, who's going to cook for you? (*Sternly*) Paride you'll have to take care of your brothers. I can't spend my whole life taking care of you! (*Speaking to the guests*) But what were they thinking, these three good-for-nothings? I'm a grown woman. If I wait any longer to get married, I'll turn into an spinster. I know how to do everything: I can cook, I can clean, I'm good at doing the wash, I always separate it by color: whites with whites and reds with reds, otherwise they bleed. I can iron, I can wash the stairs outside the house, I can give good gifts. Once a week I clean the light fixtures and once a month I clean inside the closets.

NINA *picks up the sash with the cross and hands it to* TORUCCIO.

Toruccio, can you put this on me? (*Pause*) I do everything I'm ordered.

TORUCCIO *fastens the sash over* NINA's *belly.*

(*Still speaking to her guests*) The priest gave us this sash. Because this baby is a saint! This baby is the gift I'll give my husband. (*Pause*) I'm tired! Ugh…

TORUCCIO:
Go sit down.

NINA *slumps on the chair-throne and lets her brothers fix her veil and flowers. She's visibly tired, heavy, worn out but, as her three brothers adjust her veil, she keeps sending them smiles and loving looks.*

NINA:
I'd like some strawberries!

Pause

I'd like some strawberries!

PARIDE seizes his chance and, taking advantage of NINA's wish, tells IGNAZIO to fulfill it.

PARIDE (*to IGNAZIO*):
Your sister has cravings.

Pause
IGNAZIO doesn't move.

(*authoritative*) Ignazio, go buy some strawberries for your sister!

IGNAZIO, after a moment of hesitation, puts on his coat and leaves.
Pause

NINA:
With whipped cream!

Pause

PARIDE:
Toruccio, did you hear her?

Pause

...so go!

TORUCCIO *puts on his coat and leaves.*
Pause

NINA:
I'd like a hug, please!

PARIDE *tickles her belly, kisses her on the lips, and then lowers the wedding veil over her face.*

NINA:
My husband loves me, right Paride?

PARIDE:
He loves you.

NINA:
He is thin, isn't he?

PARIDE:
Yes.

NINA:
Is he going to buy me clothes?

PARIDE:
Yes.

NINA:
And furniture too?

PARIDE:
Yes.

Pause

NINA:
Our house is in the city, right?

PARIDE:
Yes, yes!

NINA:
And is it far from the village?

PARIDE:
Not that far!

Pause
PARIDE takes a hammer and nails NINA's veil to the stage. NINA, desperate, becomes delirious.

NINA (*to the guests*):
My brothers arranged this wedding for me. They take care of me, truly!
What would I do without them, huh?

(*TO PARIDE*) My husband is handsome, because looks also matter, isn't that how the saying goes, Ignazio?

Pause
She speaks to her brothers, as if they were all right next to her.

This baby is a saint. My husband is a saint. He told Paride! Toruccio is a good boy, it's already the third time that he wants to get out.
My brothers respect me, that's why I brought them here. Jeeee... how many seagulls!
They're all dead.

PARIDE moves toward the exit keeping his eyes low and his hands in his pockets.

It's you, Toruccio! He he he! I hold him back and he goes to sleep.
That's Graziella! Jeee... how mean she was! As soon as you took the black sash from the pantry: bam! She'd whack your belly hard... It's moving, dad! It's moving, daddy! My God, I am heartily sorry for having offended you, and I detest all my sins...
Where did you get these pictures, Nina, we haven't seen them for centuries! (*Screaming*) Paride! (*PARIDE stops.*) Take them back home!

PARIDE leaves, abandoning the bride at the altar. NINA stands up and chases him, but the veil pulls her, hinders her. She's tangled. To set her free, it'd be enough to remove the clip attached to the veil from her hair, but the delirious girl keeps spinning on herself. Like a leash, the veil twists around her neck shortening her reach.
Resigned, she returns to the chair and curls up on it. She opens her eyes wide, lifts them to the sky, and smells the blinding flowers.

Without a whimper, she stands on the throne and, pulling hard on the veil that, like a noose, wraps around her neck, she hangs herself while rising from the earth toward the sky.

In a last muscular contraction, a terrible and uncontrolled spasm, NINA throws her bouquet of withered flowers at the guests, leaving imprinted in their eyes the sacred image of a martyr-bride enclosed in a religious shrine.

Life of Mine

◆

"Wer hat uns also umgedreht, daß wir,
was wir auch tun, in jener Haltung sind
von einem, welcher fortgeht? Wie er auf
dem letzten Hügel, der ihm ganz sein Tal
noch einmal zeigt, sich wendet, anhält, weilt –,
so leben wir und nehmen immer Abschied."

— RAINER MARIA RILKE
from "Die Achte Elegie"
in *Duineser Elegien*

We enter an empty room with a bed in the middle.

'What's that bed?' we ask ourselves: A shelter? A lazy respite? A terminus?

There's a temporal and spatial journey taking place around that catafalque and what moves everything is something we can't understand. The room we enter is the place where the soul lingers for a moment before tearing itself free from the body.

Sweetly, sadly, a mother eyes the three sons before her and teaches them that life is the most precious thing, it is something fleeting, it passes by. Life is a race around that bed.

Life of Mine is a foolish, desperate attempt to hold out, until all strength's vanished, that last lap before death.

Who is the chosen one? Whose turn is it? The eldest or the youngest? The best or the worst? And above all, why will it happen to someone who's not yet ready, who has not stopped, who still holds on to impulses, ideas, discoveries, projects, small charges of energy?

Among Gaspare, Uccio, and Chicco, there is a dead man who must occupy that bed, but the mother doesn't want to know; she staggers, sits down, inclines her head to one side, and looks at them one by one, her men of the house: the eldest, the middle one, the youngest... How can she feel him *hers*, that dead son? With what courage will she carry him in her arms to that bed readied for mourning, after having dressed him and whispered words of love in his ear? How will her legs not give in unexpectedly?

Everything is still: gestures, memories, words of comfort, regrets, that last rhythmic pulse of the heart repeating itself to infinity.

Life of Mine is a vigil.

That bed is a stone ship and that room is the sea that sucks us under and disappears.

— EMMA DANTE

Life of Mine premiered in October 2004 at Villa Medici in Rome as part of Romaeuropa Festival. It was produced by Romaeuropa Festival and Compagnia Sud Costa Occidentale directed by Emma Dante. The people who immersed themselves in this tragedy are Ersilia Lombardo (The Mother), Giacomo Guarnieri (Chicco), Alessio Piazza (Uccio), and Vincenzo Di Michele (Gaspare).

CHARACTERS:

THE MOTHER

The Sons:

GASPARE
The eldest

UCCIO
The middle child

CHICCO
The youngest

In the center of the room there's a bed on which lies a crucifix. Those invited to the vigil enter the space and sit in a semicircle around the bed. CHICCO *races around on his bicycle, an old, beat up, rusty Graziella, while* THE MOTHER *and the two brothers, hands in their pockets, stand close to the bed and, with their eyes, follow the spectators who slowly take their seats.* CHICCO *pedals fast, slows down, zig-zags, brakes abruptly, and smiles blissfully.* THE MOTHER, *dressed in mourning, keeps an eye on him and cries silently when he looks at her. The three young men wear pajamas and gym shoes.*

CHICCO (*suddenly breaking*):
It's late, mama!

THE MOTHER:
Hush! Did you want the bicycle? Now, ride it!

CHICCO *pedals and laps around faster.*

UCCIO:
We've got to hurry, mà!

THE MOTHER:
Do you think I like this?! I said you've got to be quiet, you've got to be quiet all three of you! Understood?

GASPARE:
But why, was I talking?

THE MOTHER:
And aren't you talking now? Who told you to speak? Quiet!

The bicycle circles around the bed. The audience can hear the creaking of the chain and the generator that, scraping the front wheel, produces electricity for the headlight. After a few seconds, CHICCO *gets closer to the head of the bed, stops, and waits along with the others.*

UCCIO (*to* CHICCO):
Can I go for a spin on the bike?

THE MOTHER *springs up, furious, and with a hop unloads a slap onto* UCCIO's *head.*

UCCIO:
Ahh!!! No, mà, I was kidding!

THE MADRE:
I told you to be quiet!

THE MOTHER *looks at the three brothers with disdain, sits at the foot of the bed and puts them to shame pitilessly in front of the guests.*

THE MOTHER (*turning her back to her sons who remain standing, their heads hanging*):
I wanted a girl! If I'd told a little girl to be quiet, wouldn't she have stayed quiet? (*She nods repeatedly, answering the question herself.*) She'd have been quiet, she'd have been quiet! Instead with the three of them it doesn't happen, because I tell them one thing and they let it in one ear and out the other! It's like this, the whole damn day! I can't take it anymore! (*She turns and notices that* CHICCO *is sitting on the bed.*) Get up!

CHICCO *immediately stands up and sits on the bicycle's saddle.*

124

They don't listen to me! They don't want to hear anything, they're only good at leaving dirty underwear around the house, socks on top of the closet, dirty cups left and right…

GASPARE:
Mamà, does this seem like the right time to tell people these things?

THE MOTHER:
And when should I tell people these things, when they leave? Now I have to tell them, now, that they've come to visit us! This way they'll know how you treat me. (*Reprovingly pointing at* GASPARE) This one! This one this one… is the eldest. His name is Gaspare. Now, one might ask: being that he's the eldest shouldn't he bring a little something home to his mother? (*She nods repeatedly, answering the question herself.*) I really think he should bring a little something! And so I tell him: "Blood of mine, go work, go look for a teeny-weeny job… Something to do…".

GASPARE:
There's no work, mà!

THE MOTHER:
"There's no work" he tells me. "No job openings to be found!" "There's unemployment!" Because my darling boy would like to be… I don't know: a lawyer, an engineer, a state employee, he'd like to have cash incentives, end-of-year bonuses… that's what he'd like. And instead I tell him: "Blood of mine, make do, go be a baker, I'm not telling you to go work in the shipyards because if you fall off a ladder, since we all know they are never up to code, you'll end up dead, it's dangerous and I'd even understand that! But the ice-cream man, the illegal parking lot attendant, couldn't you do that?" And instead, what does he do? He strolls around, the whole damn day, left and right, left and right… (*Referring to* UCCIO) with this other idiot who's here at my side.

UCCIO:
It's not true, mà!

125

THE MOTHER:

How is it not true? Why where do you go all day that nobody knows anything about it? Uccio, his name is Uccio, the middle one – although I don't even like the name, who gave it to you, your grandma?

UCCIO:

What do I know, mà?

THE MOTHER:

That's right, blood of mine, you can't know! (*To the audience*) Uccio's a half-wit!

UCCIO:

You shouldn't say these things to strangers, mà!

THE MOTHER:

Why shouldn't I tell them? Isn't it the truth? Can't they all see you're a half-wit?

UCCIO:

Yes, but you shouldn't underline it, though, really!

THE MOTHER:

Don't worry, blood of mine! It's nothing!

CHICCO (*making fun of* UCCIO):

It's nothing, got it?

THE MOTHER:

…Saved the best for last: Chicco. The youngest. Now, the first two came out as God willed and that burden must be carried, but the youngest one shouldn't he give his mama something to be proud of? (*She nods repeatedly, answering the question herself*) I think he should give her the satisfaction! And so I tell him: "Blood of mine, study! Make something of yourself, become a city council member! This way you can find a job for your big brother and a disability pension for Uccio, poor soul!"

CHICCO:
But why, to be a councilperson one has to study, mà?

THE MOTHER:
But open a book, look at how it's made, pretend you're reading and look at the pictures instead, lie to my face! And instead, what does he do? The whole damn day on that bike… He's going to make my heart burst! Because I'm scared of these things! He's such a rascal he rides it even around the house. Ruined all my furniture, bumping into stuff everywhere. I've got animals inside my house! How is this life? I'm tired! I can't take it anymore!

GASPARE:
Get up, mamà, we've got to get it ready!

THE MOTHER closes her eyes and, using her hands to feel her way, looks for the crucifix on the bed.
She picks it up, stands up, and, speaking softly, slowly moves toward the spectators.

THE MOTHER:
Yet, all three are my life! All three! But what would I do without them? And them without me, where would they go? They're three boys, they're young! I don't say it to them, otherwise give them a hand and they'll take the whole arm! But I am proud of my sons, I'm proud of how I brought them up, because I raised them, alone, no-one helped me. And if someone dares to speak ill of one of them, I'll pulverize them! Because only I can speak ill of my sons! Only I know that when they'll grow up they'll become three righteous men! Because all three are my heart! All three are my life!

CHICCO *lets go of the bicycle and is about to throw himself on the bed. The brothers stop him and, gesturing toward the catafalque to ward off bad luck, they try to convince him to keep his distance.* CHICCO *doesn't care, he takes a running start and speeds off.* GASPARE *anticipates him.*

GASPARE (*screaming*):
Chicco!

THE MOTHER *suddenly turns around and sees* GASPARE *lying on the bed.*

THE MOTHER:
Noooo!

UCCIO *and* CHICCO *lift up the bed and unload* GASPARE *off it, making him roll onto the floor. In turn, the three brothers lie down on the catafalque and play dead, their bodies rigid. They throw themselves on the bed, do summersaults, roll and jump in a frenzied steeplechase. They look like shrapnel fragments.* THE MOTHER *beats her chest, kisses the crucifix and collapses three times. She stands and she falls, stands and falls, stands and falls... Her legs give way at that horrid spectacle: the bed attracts her sons inexorably, like a magnet.*
THE MOTHER *is driven back by gusts of wind and, when she finally manages to reach the catafalque, she capsizes it, empties it, and chases away her sons. Suddenly, the hex is broken.*

THE MOTHER (*furious*):
I don't like this game! Good-for-nothings!!! Move away... quickly... Otherwise I'll kill you, you understood? You shouldn't play with these things, you crooks! Godless sons, you are! Move away... Go take a walk! Get out of my sight, you've undone everything!

THE MOTHER plumps up the mattress, straightens the bedspread, and before hooking the crucifix to the headboard, she blesses her sons. GASPARE and UCCIO move away, tails between their legs. CHICCO picks up the bicycle and, after tripping UCCIO, he pedals round and round the bed. GASPARE slaps CHICCO on the head to punish him.

THE MOTHER (*while she's putting things in order*):
Good-for-nothings!

UCCIO:
That'll learn you, Chicco!

THE MOTHER:
Godless, you are! Godless!

CHICCO (*to GASPARE*):
Didn't hurt me at all!

GASPARE (*to CHICCO*):
That didn't do it? Do you want another one?

THE MOTHER:
Three useless things, you are!

UCCIO:
You shouldn't trip me, Chicco!

THE MOTHER:
Good at nothing!

UCCIO:
Because otherwise I'll hurt myself, I, really!

THE MOTHER:
Good-for-nothings, you're killing me! I'll call the cops and I'll get you arrested. Useless things! I'll lock you up in boarding school, with the priests, that way you'll understand what it means to live without your mother. I'm young, it's not like I can die taking care of you! Are you listening?

GASPARE and UCCIO, *hands in pockets, stroll around in a circle.* CHICCO *follows them on his bike. From under the bed,* THE MOTHER *takes out a drawer with what is necessary for the funeral preparations: a white veil, ten candles for the dead, a shirt, a pair of trousers, a jacket, a neck tie. Everything is rigorously white, spotless and immaculate. The three brothers observe this sad ritual in silence.*
When THE MOTHER *shakes out the shirt, which had been stored in that drawer for God knows how long, a few confetti flutter about.*

UCCIO:
Mama, that's my shirt!

THE MOTHER:
Now it's your brother's! You don't need it!

THE MOTHER *carefully folds and sets on the bed the white suit for the deceased.*

UCCIO:
I wore that shirt for Carnival when I dressed up as Zorro!

GASPARE:
Yeah, with a flabby hat and without a sword!

THE MOTHER:
Carnival is over!

UCCIO:
You took my sword and even poked my eye out, remember?

THE MOTHER:
Good-for-nothings, this stuff is all you think about!

UCCIO:
But why do they always have to touch my stuff, mà?

THE MOTHER:
Do you think I like this?! Don't you get it that this isn't the time to think about these things? I can't listen to you anymore! You get under my skin!

THE MOTHER puts the candles on the empty drawer that now functions as a nightstand at the head of the bed. But things keep falling out of her hands. She's in despair. CHICCO calls her to distract her.

CHICCO:
Mama? Do you remember when you dressed us up as the Three Musketeers for Carnival?

THE MOTHER:
Yes, blood of mine.

UCCIO:
Athos. Aramìs…

CHICCO:
And D'Artagnàn.

UCCIO:
Because you were the youngest!

CHICCO:
The best! What happened to the Three Musketeers, mà?

THE MOTHER:
They're put away.

UCCIO:
Even Aramìs?

THE MOTHER:
Sè![29]

CHICCO:
And Uccio, all dressed up as Aramìs, but instead of a white horse he had a hamster, do you remember, mà?

THE MOTHER:
I remember...

CHICCO:
One fine day, Uccio, out of nowhere comes home with the hamster in a cage all wrapped in a bow, because he said that Aramìs, to be a true musketeer, needed a horse!

UCCIO:
Porthos, I called him. You don't know this, but to make Porthos exercise, I tied him to the plastic wheel and spun it with my finger. He was good at it, mà!

THE MOTHER lights the candles.

CHICCO:
Gaspare, what was the veranda of our old house like?

GASPARE:
Long.

CHICCO:
And what was at the end of the veranda, Uccio?

UCCIO:
A wall.

CHICCO:
And Uccio who, after having trained Porthos, takes the cage, puts it on the veranda, opens the door, and to the hamster is like: "Gallop, gallop!?"

UCCIO:
Ride Porthos!

They double over with laughter.

CHICCO:
And this tiny rat-thing starts to walk real slow at first, and then faster and faster, faster and faster... He thought he was on the wheel, poor thing... and at some point: SPLAT! He made a splash... on the wall?! Ended up dying like a rat, mà...

THE MOTHER looks at her sons with infinite tenderness. Then opens her arms toward CHICCO.

THE MOTHER:
It's late! Come here... come!

CHICCO *hands the bicycle to* GASPARE *and runs to hug his mother.* GASPARE *unscrews a bolt, folds the Graziella bicycle in half and rests it against the wall in a corner of the room.*

THE MOTHER:
Now mom'll dress you nice. Come!

THE MOTHER *makes* CHICCO *sit at the foot of the bed, takes off his pajamas. With a broken heart, she's about to dress him for the wake.* CHICCO *is cheerful, lively, unknowing… in her eyes, he is alive.*

THE MOTHER (*taking off his gym shoes*):
These shoes are old, Chicco.

CHICCO:
They're the shoes I play soccer in, mà!

THE MOTHER:
I know, blood of mine! You're attached to these shoes, but now you have to take them off, you understand me?

CHICCO *shakes his foot uncontrollably fast.*

THE MOTHER:
Stop moving, Chicco, stop!

CHICCO:
The shoe, it moves on its own, mà. It's used to juggling a ball…

THE MOTHER:
I know, blood of mine…

CHICCO:
65, 74, 2000, 6000 juggles with this shoe on my foot.

CHICCO *lets himself be dragged around by the shoe, which runs behind an invisible ball.*

THE MOTHER:
Stop, Chicco! Grab him Uccio!

UCCIO *chases* CHICCO *and tries to stop him.*

CHICCO:
The good stuff is when Uccio wants to take the ball away from me, which means even Speedy Gonzales can't!

UCCIO *catches him and brings him back to his mother.*

That's a foul, though, Uccio! Yellow card!

THE MOTHER:
Sit down!

THE MOTHER, *crying, hugs him, kisses him, rubs against him and, in the meanwhile, dresses him.*

135

CHICCO:
Mama, want to know something nice? The Palermo is in Serie A.

THE MOTHER:
Yes, blood of mine!

CHICCO:
Didn't I pass the ball to Toni Goal?[30]

He runs away again.

THE MOTHER:
Chicco stop! Come here!

CHICCO:
I was in the bleachers and saw how the whole play happened: I had this shoe on my foot and I went down to the field myself; and I started to mark the sweeper, the midfielder, the midfield anchor, the forward…

THE MOTHER (*while she chases after* CHICCO):
Gaspare, get me the shirt, hurry!

CHICCO:
…at some point I saw that Toni Goal was in the penalty area and I was about to cross…

THE MOTHER *blocks him and he picks her up.*

THE MOTHER:
Put me down, Chicco!

CHICCO:

…but there was this great defender called mamà and I couldn't.

THE MOTHER holds his head tight between her hands and she lays it on her chest. She laughs and cries. Simultaneously. It's excruciating. She puts the shirt on him and tries to button it up, but she can't: the buttons don't fit the buttonholes.

THE MOTHER:

Chicco, mom's hands are shaking today.

CHICCO:

When I grow up, I'll button up my shirt myself, mà!

CHICCO wriggles free and, running, fastens the shirt himself. THE MOTHER chases after him.

THE MOTHER:

Chicco I told you to hold still!

CHICCO:

Make that one day I have to go out with my girlfriend…

THE MOTHER:

I told you that mom's tired today, stop… Come here!

CHICCO:

…what am I going to do, call you from the veranda: "Mama, hey, can you button up my shirt?" As if? How would that look to my girl!

THE MOTHER (*screaming*):
Chicco come here, or I'll slaughter you!

Obediently, CHICCO *goes back to his mother. As he ran, he inserted the buttons in the wrong buttonholes. The shirt is all twisted.*

(*With infinite tenderness*) Do you see, you can't fasten up a shirt by yourself? You're young, life of mine!

THE MOTHER *fixes the buttons and bends down to help him put on his pants.*

My back hurts!

CHICCO *stands on the bed to allow his mother to buckle his belt without bending over. While he caresses her hair, he looks at her with love from above.*

CHICCO:
Mama, why don't you put on that pretty dress, the one I like, and let your hair down, that way you'll get rid of all this sadness in your eyes!

THE MOTHER:
Yes, blood of mine! First, though, I have to dress you! (*She picks up the tie*) Look what I'm putting on you!...

CHICCO:
But what's that dangly thing, mà?

THE MOTHER:
A tie!

CHICCO:
And what's it for?

THE MOTHER:
It makes you look sharp!

The jacket, and he's ready. Ecstatic, THE MOTHER *looks at him: he's an angel dressed in white.*
In the meanwhile, the other two brothers have remained seated on the bed with their elbows on their knees and their hands covering their faces. They uncover their eyes and smile through tears at their brother. CHICCO *responds with a sudden gesture of joy: he takes a running start and leaps into his mother's arms.*

CHICCO (*singing a soccer stadium anthem*):
Toni Goal! Toni Goal! We don't care about Del Piero, 'cause we have our Toni Goal. Toni Goal! Toni Goal!

He holds her tight.

THE MOTHER:
Let go, Chicco. Let go! Don't cling so tight, I'll fall... I can't hold you any-more. I can't take it... Let go, life of mine!

THE MOTHER *splits away from him. She spins him around to avoid looking at his face, pushes him toward the bed, and gives him an encouraging pat on his rear.*

Lie down!!!

CHICCO *lies down. Assuming the posture of a corpse, he slowly falls asleep with his hands crossed on his chest. He is stiff, still, lifeless.* THE MOTHER *lowers a black veil over her face and cries and prays at her son's bedside, staring at the crucifix.*

(*In a whisper*) Cover him!

The brothers are about to cover the corpse with a white lace veil, when, suddenly, THE MOTHER *stops them.*

Wait! Leave him with me for a bit!

The two don't listen to her and continue to cover him.

Uccio, wait! I said: leave him with me for a bit!

UCCIO:
Mama, Chicco is…

THE MOTHER:
Shut up!

GASPARE:
He can't move anymore, mamà!

THE MOTHER:
You're wrong. He's moving!

THE MOTHER *throws herself on her dead son and shakes him, trying to reanimate him. She does so energetically, imparting momentum to his body, which bounces on the bed. By inertia,* CHICCO *follows the tremors generated by this external force but since his body is inclined to stay still, the movement slowly ceases.*

Move, Chicco! Like this! That's right! No! Don't stop!
Chicco, when your mother tells you to do something, you have to do it, you hear me?
Come on, show them you can move... Move, life of mine... Move!

THE MOTHER *doesn't give up. She shakes him harder, begging him to not stop moving. Exasperated, she doubles the rhythm of the jolts she gives the mattress and the body bounces off it.* CHICCO *comes to and dies off. Comes to and dies off, until* GASPARE *brutally grabs his mother and yanks her away from the bed.*

GASPARE:
Think, mamà, think! Who are you showing this to?! It's over, do you understand?! It's over. Leave him alone, mà! Don't torment him. He can't move anymore, you understand? This is life. We have to let him go. He has to stay there, in bed, and there's nothing else to be done...

UCCIO (*screaming*):
Gaspare?

GASPARE *and* THE MOTHER *suddenly turn around.*

(*Without taking his eyes off of* CHICCO) He's moving!

We hear the squeaking of the bed springs but CHICCO *seems motionless.*
THE MOTHER *and* GASPARE *stare at him fixedly but only when their
eyes look more carefully they catch a glimpse in his seemingly rigid chest of the
imperceptible pulsing of his heart.*

THE MOTHER:
That's right! That's right! (*To* GASPARE) Can't you see he's moving?
(*To* CHICCO) Like this! Move, blood of mine! Don't stop... Get out of
this bed for the dead! What's this bed have to do with you? You're a little
boy!

Miraculously, CHICCO *comes back to life. In a rhythmic crescendo, he
bounces off the bed, he opens his eyes, he unfolds his hands and his body
loosens up...*
*The deceased dances a sirtaki and his heart skips in his chest. It pounds, beats,
quivers...*
The brothers and THE MOTHER *festively circle around his whirling bed
doing tumbles and cartwheels, somersaults and pirouettes like merry acrobats*

UCCIO:
He's moving, Gaspare!

GASPARE:
Shut up! (*To his mother*) Mà, stop!

THE MOTHER:
Move! That's right, that's right! Like this! Don't stop, Chicco!
(*To* GASPARE) Can't you see he's moving? Help me you two!

UCCIO:
Chicco, relax your hands!

GASPARE:
What relax your hands? But then you're completely stupid! Stop, Chicco! He can't move anymore, mama… We have to let him go! Won't you understand? He has to stay there, in bed! That's his place.

THE MOTHER:
Don't stop! Get out of this bed of death!

UCCIO:
He's moving, Gaspare!

GASPARE (*unable to continue to deny what is apparent*):
Mamà, he's really moving!

THE MOTHER:
Didn't I tell you he moved?

GASPARE:
But is this real?

UCCIO:
It's real! Get up, Chicco!

THE MOTHER:
Get uuuup!!!

GASPARE:
Ride one last time…he's moving, mà!

THE MOTHER:
Didn't I tell you he moooveeed?

CHICCO *gets out of the bed and, in his last ride on the merry-go-round, he detaches himself from his soul.*

UCCIO *chases after him, festive and foolish;* THE MOTHER *begs him to keep going;* GASPARE *takes the bicycle and, without screwing on the bolt, offers it to* CHICCO *with the hope of bringing him back to life, to usual, everyday life. But* CHICCO *dashes off, runs… he's alive and beside himself with happiness.*
When UCCIO *catches him and clasps him close,* CHICCO *languidly slips away from him. And, after he crushes against the bicycle that, like a magnet, is reunited with him, the handlebars thrust through his chest.*
Time rewinds to the precise instant when CHICCO *lost his life. Everything is in its place:* THE MOTHER *kneels in front of the lifeless body of her son who is lying on the ground next to the bent and dented Graziella.*

THE MOTHER (*looking around her with crazed eyes*):
Uccio, I'd almost forgotten the flowers!

In a corner of the room there's a red rose bush, the last decorative element needed for the funeral preparations. Between the branches of the plant rests a red sash camouflaged among the roses. THE MOTHER *takes off her black veil and lets down her hair, looking at* CHICCO *with a strange smile.*

Gaspare, tidy up the bed for me!

GASPARE *plumps up the mattress and tucks in the bedspread.*

Turn your backs, I have to get dressed. (*She takes off the black dress.*) I don't need this anymore. What's with this black stuff?

THE MOTHER *positions the bush at the head of the bed, takes the red sash, and unrolls it: a very elegant red evening dress magically appears.*

144

Looks like new! Who knows if it still fits.
I'll put it on!
This way I'll get rid of all this sadness in my eyes! Beautiful, isn't it?!
(*She puts on the red dress.*) Uccio, zip me up! (*UCCIO zips her up.*)
(*To* GASPARE *and* UCCIO) Go to bed, it's late!

Kneeling, THE MOTHER *goes back to* CHICCO, *she kisses him, and lifts him up holding him by the waist.*
She puts her son's heels on the tips of her feet and, to keep him upright and glued to herself, she walks backward supporting his weight with her whole body.

Get this bicycle out of my sight!

UCCIO:
Can I have it, mà? Or are you giving it to Gaspare?

THE MOTHER *is stunning in her bright evening dress and, clutching her prince, she drags him around in a melancholic and heart-wrenching dance.*

THE MOTHER:
You're a half-wit, Uccio, but your mother loves you. I can't give you the bike because otherwise you'll get hurt! You'll get hurt!!!

THE MOTHER *lies down on the bed, carefully laying her dead son on top of her.*

Shroud us!

GASPARE, *embarrassed, moves closer to the bed and, looking at the audience out of the corner of his eye, speaks to his mother with reproach and shame.*

GASPARE:
Get up, ma! Everyone's looking at us!

THE MOTHER:
I said, cover me up!

UCCIO *springs forward and obeys the command: using the veil, he covers the two bodies clasped in the incest of death.*

GASPARE:
What are you doing?

UCCIO:
She told me to cover her up and I'm covering her!

GASPARE:
But then you're completely stupid, right?
Mama, tell him you were joking. Otherwise he'll really believe it!

UCCIO:
Gaspare Calafiore be a sensible little boy! (*Pause*) Mama? (*Pause*) Is this how it ends, mà? You'll just leave us here like two idiots in pajamas, with all these people looking at us?

GASPARE *laughs hysterically.*

THE MOTHER:
Lie down, Uccio. It's late!

146

GASPARE laughs even more.

UCCIO:
What are you laughing at?

GASPARE (*making fun of him*):
Lie down!

UCCIO (*sneering while pointing at the bed*):
It's true I'm a half-wit, but there's no more space here, right?

GASPARE:
It's a single bed, mà! We can't all fit!

UCCIO:
He he he! We don't fit, Gaspare!

GASPARE:
Wait, I have an idea!

He takes off his shoes.

UCCIO:
What are you doing?

GASPARE:
Mama!?

GASPARE lifts the veil and tries to get in bed with his mother and brother.

THE MOTHER (*shooing him*):
Get out!

GASPARE *and* UCCIO *play and joke around like when they were kids.*

UCCIO:
What an ass, you really make me laugh!

GASPARE:
I don't fit in here!

UCCIO:
Gaspare, lie down under the bed and tickle Chicco. Under the mattress…
Come on, scare him… Like when we were little!

GASPARE *shakes the mattress while getting under the bed.*

GASPARE:
Chicco, an earthquake is coming!

UCCIO:
He he he, he makes me laugh so hard… what an ass!

He can't see GASPARE *anymore and is frightened.*

Where are you? Did you leave me alone?

THE MOTHER:
Gaspare, don't move the bed!

UCCIO:
I don't want to stay here by myself! Don't leave me alone, I get scared!
Mama?! Mama?!

UCCIO is about to start crying when he notices the bicycle and has an idea.

GASPARE:
Uccio, look what I found down here!

From underneath the bed GASPARE throws out masks, streamers, and confetti.

THE MOTHER:
Gaspare, leave them here!

UCCIO (*putting on a mask*):
Jeee, my Zorro mask!

GASPARE:
Chicco!?? (*Playing a party horn*) Pew pew pew pew pew pew!!!

THE MOTHER:
Good-for-nothings! Carnival's over!

GASPARE:
Uccio, here, you play it for Chicco!

He throws the party horn to UCCIO.

UCCIO:
Chicco, don't let mama get up, I'm taking the bicycle for a spin.

THE MOTHER (*scolding him*):
Uccio, don't you dare touch that bicycle! You'll hurt yourself!

UCCIO:
No, mà, I'll be fine!

UCCIO takes the bicycle and, without mounting on the saddle, he begins to push it rapidly around the bed.

THE MOTHER (*screaming*):
Uccio, I said: leave that bicycle alone.

UCCIO:
I won't get on it, mama. I'm pushing it, since I don't know how to ride it anyway…

THE MOTHER:
Gaspare, help me with your brother, take that bicycle away from him, before he gets hurt!

GASPARE (*to UCCIO*):
Did you want the bicycle? Now, ride it!

THE MOTHER:
Gaspare, I can't get up! Take that bicycle away from him because if he falls he'll break his head!

GASPARE:
He's got a thick skull, mamà, he won't get hurt, don't worry!

UCCIO:
Gaspare, say, should I go for a ride?

GASPARE:
Run Zorro, run!

THE MOTHER:
Uccio, stop, I don't like this game!

UCCIO toots the horn and GASPARE throws confetti and streamers, which fall on the bed colorfully and festively. The catafalque becomes a Viareggio carnival float.

Godless you are, godless!
Uccio, if I get up, I'm going to slaughter you!

UCCIO:
Mamà, my head's spinning!

THE MOTHER:
Uccio I'm getting up, Uccio! I'm up...

THE MOTHER throws her legs and arms about and, ready to spring up, she lifts her head stunning her idiot child with a withering look. UCCIO freezes, terrified. THE MOTHER clasps CHICCO's hands so as to not let him fall, then throws a shoe at UCCIO and points at the foot of the bed with her naked foot.

Put, that bicycle here, at the foot of the bed, immediately. Move it, you idiot! Not a half-wit, you're a complete idiot!

UCCIO *obeys: he folds the Grazziella and puts it at the foot of the bed.*

Here, I want to touch it with my foot.

She kicks off the other shoe and slips her foot between the spokes of a wheel to keep it under control.

This way... I'm the only one who can touch this bicycle, got it? Cover everything up and go lie down!

After he also covers the bicycle with the veil, UCCIO *hangs his mask on the crucifix and slips under the bed. Now they're all inside the catafalque.*

Good-for-nothings! I can't leave you alone not even for a minute. You have no self-control, like little children... You're killing me. I can't take it anymore. Good-for-nothings! I'll call the cops and I'll get you arrested. Useless things! I'll lock you up in boarding school, with the priests, that way you'll understand what it means to live without your mother. I'm young, it's not like I can die taking care of you! Are you listening? (*Pause*) Useless things... (*Pause*)

THE MOTHER's *nervous foot vigorously pushes the bicycle wheel, which begins to spin.*
The bed seems to be moving. One push, then another, and the wheel won't stop anymore.
Lulled by the squeaking of the chain, THE MOTHER *and the sons slip off into a slumber.*

But…
…all three of you are my life…
…all three…

In the darkness the flames of the candles flicker uncertainly.

Market Dogs

◆

Market Dogs

◆

Facts and characters here recounted are fictional.
Any resemblance to real individuals is theatrically coincidental.

"Truth is at the bottom of a well: look inside a well and you see the sun or the moon; but if you throw yourself in, there's no more sun or moon, just the truth."[31]

— LEONARDO SCIASCIA
from *The Day of the Owl*

The mafia is a woman-bitch who shows her teeth before opening her thighs. She heads a pack of sons who, wagging their tails, get in line to kiss her. Her kiss is Honor. The bitch gives her sons permission to enter: "In the name of the Father, the Son, the Mother and the Holy Spirit." She clobbers her youngest son and dresses him in a suit stained with blood. The *mafioso* is reborn and blessed by the Mother. His brothers embrace him and demand an oath: "I enter with blood and I'll leave in blood." The pact is sealed.

This is how I reimagine the affiliation ritual of a man who, swearing before God, gives himself forever to the mafia. This ancient rite is folklore, it is the postcard-ready mafia found in an agritourism venue in the Corleone countryside where people eat ricotta and chicory and pray along with Radio Maria.

But folklore is a lavishly decked table that helps hide the horror and behind which, hidden from people's eyes, takes place something that can't be spoken, that doesn't even make the news. The mafia is the triumph of lies, it is the wrong side becoming the right one, the underbelly floating to the surface, the low becoming high, crime turning into law.

A clan, a fish trap, a political party, a company, a brotherhood: a Family.

One can end up in this corral by birth, for fear, or for love. Those who enter it incur eternal obligations. The bonds become indissoluble, the pacts unbreakable. They can't back out, they can't go back. It is a savage belonging, herd-like. Those who leave the herd die.

In Sicily lives a people that speaks a secret jargon, accompanied by winks, by gestures made with hands, heads, eyes, shoulders, bellies, feet. A people capable of making a whole speech without ever opening their mouths.

This people has a mafioso-like attitude that has nothing to do with the mafia. For example: I'm driving down a narrow one-way street and a car going the wrong way appears in front of me. I stop, I'm in a hurry, and I honk my horn.

I wait for the driver to move backward but, despite my courage, one look and a movement of her head are enough to make me understand that I'd better back away. I don't think that the driver of that car is a mafiosa, even though her attitude is. It is easier to meet a contemporary mafioso in a government-owned car in Rome's city center, in the correct direction of travel.

The mafia woman-bitch disgusts herself and asks her children to disown her. She pushes them away to not soil their name; she is a whore who is ashamed of her past. She fed them with the blood of innocent victims, she sent them to school, she ennobled them. Now her children have become important. They fill the highest offices. The bitch offers her children an upside-down, divided Italy, made of "little islands not controlled by anyone." In this new map, Sicily is in the north. The bitch doesn't worry anymore about punishing the truth, the one that cost Peppino Impastato his life, because she managed to delegitimize this truth, discrediting judicial authorities and accustoming public opinion to illegality.

In an island in the north of an upside-down Italy there is a *madrice* city,[32] a primal place, where a silent people, sitting around a lavishly decked table, divvies up Italy and eats its raw flesh.

— EMMA DANTE

CHARACTERS
in hierarchical order:

MAMMASANTISSIMA
Or, The Sacred Mother; Sicilian

TOTÒ SICILIANO
a.k.a. "UNCLE TOTÒ the Scalpel"; Sicilian

SALVATORE SPAGNUOLO
a.k.a. "DON SASÀ"; from Campania

TONI CINTOLA
a.k.a. "BIG JIM"; Sicilian

GIROLAMO RICCIO
a.k.a. "GEGÈ the Chemist"; from Campania

STEFANO VARVARÁ
a.k.a. "SLIM FAST"; Sicilian

GENNARO PANZANELLA
a.k.a. "JOKER"; Sicilian

GIUSEPPE BONANNO
a.k.a. "DAGGER"; Sicilian

VITO MONTALTO
a.k.a. "The MOUSE"; Sicilian

FEDERICO PANUNZIO
a.k.a. "The DOORMAN"; Sicilian

LIBORIO PAGLINO
A train conductor, from Campania

LIBORIO PAGLINO, *a railway worker, stands on the proscenium line in* *front of* SALVATORE SPAGNUOLO, *a.k.a.* DON SASÀ. DON SASÀ, *blindfolded, lies on the ground in his underwear. He looks dead. Roughly* *ten wooden plate stands are lined up before* LIBORIO, *each of them hold-* *ing an image of the Immaculate Conception. A votive candle sits in front of* *each image. A colorful map made of arrows, numbers, and circles adorns the* *stage... it brings to mind a board game, the game of Mafiopoli. Next to a red* *circle there's the outline of a body where those who are punched or butt-headed* *usually fall to the ground.*

Upstage, the market dogs get dressed behind the backrests of eleven chairs of *different heights, arranged in ascending order. At their center, the tallest chair* *of all:* MAMMASANTISSIMA's *throne. The dogs wear double-breasted* *linen suits, vibrantly colored ties, and colorful wide-brimmed floppy hats.* *Their lips are painted red.* MAMMASANTISSIMA, *dressed like one of* *them, stands on her throne, her back to the audience. When the dogs are* *ready,* FEDERICO PANUNZIO, *a.k.a. "The* DOORMAN," *comes forward* *and begins to light the candles starting from stage left and making his way* *toward stage right. After lighting the first two candles, he carefully observes* LIBORIO. LIBORIO *reciprocates his look from behind the glasses that rest* *on his nose.*

PANUNZIO:
Can you see?

LIBORIO:
Yes.

PANUNZIO:
Are you sure?

LIBORIO:
Without any problem whatsoever.

PANUNZIO gets back to lighting the candles. When he is done, he addresses LIBORIO to begin his interrogation.

PANUNZIO:
Liborio Paglino, you were born on December 25th, 1966 in San Bartolomeo in Galdo, province of Benevento.

LIBORIO:
Santissimini Gerolomini St., number 2.

PANUNZIO:
You're single, you have no children, no relatives, and you suffer from a severe vision impairment, correct?

LIBORIO:
Minus eight diopters.

PANUNZIO:
You're 5 feet 5 inches tall without the hat, your shoe size is an 8 on the right side and an 8 ½ on the left, and you have no criminal record. Am I correct?

LIBORIO:
A spotlessly clean record, really.

PANUNZIO (*pointing at* DON SASÀ):
Do you recognize this man?

LIBORIO (*taking off his glasses*):
Yes.

PANUNZIO:
Are you sure?

LIBORIO (*putting on the glasses*):
Certainly.

PANUNZIO:
You're a train conductor.

LIBORIO:
Senior in my shift.

PANUNZIO:
And, customarily, your duty is to inspect tickets.

LIBORIO:
I also help travelers; let's not forget that.

PANUNZIO:
You work eight hours per day and usually you're at the tail-end of the train where you have more responsibilities.

LIBORIO:
The tail-end is the most critical section of the train.

PANUNZIO:
But you never stop moving, you aren't always at your post... you go back and forth through the corridor, a little in the tail and a little at the head.

LIBORIO:
My brief is to ensure that everything goes well, that everything is quiet, smooth. If there are problems, a criticality or disruptions, I must report them to my shift supervisor, the head conductor. who keeps to the front of the train.

PANUNZIO:
And that's what I wanted to get to, your shift supervisor, the head conductor; you usually give him the "Ready to Go" signal, am I correct?

LIBORIO:
But how do you know all this information about me?

PANUNZIO:
I am a tick.

LIBORIO takes off his glasses and observes PANUNZIO.

LIBORIO:
I wouldn't say so! Ticks are something else. They belong to the animal sort; you're sort of a man! Am I correct?

PANUNZIO:
Three years ago, at the Vibo Valenzia Pizzo Station, you gave the head conductor the "Ready to Go" and didn't see that your young colleague, a conductor on shift, still had his head under a wagon to check on a break!

LIBORIO:
It was a terrible accident! Let's just not talk about it.

PANUNZIO:
How come you didn't see him? Didn't you have your glasses on?

LIBORIO:
Of course I had them on, if not, how could I work?

PANUNZIO:
But you can't see anything with those glasses, Liborio!

LIBORIO:
What are you talking about?

PANUNZIO:
You're not missing eight diopters, your eyesight is 20/20.

LIBORIO:
Not true! That's slander, through and through.

PANUNZIO (*showing him four fingers*):
How many fingers?

LIBORIO:
Five.

PANUNZIO:
Not true! It's four, you see?

LIBORIO takes off his glasses.

PANUNZIO (*pointing at DON SASÀ*):
You obtained your job by asking this man for help. And it was he who procured for you the fake certificate of disability that forces you to wear glasses at all times.

LIBORIO:
You've got it all wrong.

PANUNZIO:
Without this fake visual impairment you wouldn't have made the list.

LIBORIO:
Slander, through and through!

PANUNZIO (*snatching* LIBORIO's *glasses*):
Because of these, you didn't see your young colleague crouching under the train nor his head rolling down the tracks ten seconds after departure.

After a silence filled with tension, LIBORIO *takes off his glasses and rubs his eyes.*

LIBORIO:
I had never settled for a compromise in my entire life, never! It wasn't my fault. I needed a job! (*Pointing at* DON SASÀ) I'd known of him for a while, he's also from San Bartolomeo in Galdo. One day, I saw him at the café in the piazza and, after telling him all my troubles, he seemed accommodating, kind... Please, don't say anything to anyone, otherwise you'll get me into trouble.

PANUNZIO:
Make the sign of the cross.

LIBORIO:
What?

PANUNZIO:
Make the sign of the cross!

LIBORIO:
In the name of the Father, the Son, and the Holy Spirit. So Be It.

PANUNZIO:
After me: in the name of the Father, the Son, the Mother, and the Holy Spirit, Amen. Repeat with me: in the name of the Father, the Son, the Mother, and the Holy Spirit, Amen.

LIBORIO:
...of the Holy Spirit, Amen.

PANUNZIO:
You're a respectable person, Liborio Paglino. Don't you worry. Put your glasses back on and keep them on, always. If you'll tell no-one what you'll hear, I swear I'll keep your secret. Can you see?

LIBORIO:
No.

PANUNZIO:
Good.

PANUNZIO turns toward MAMMASANTISSIMA and gives her the "Ready to Go" signal. Then he goes behind the chairs and shakes them together with his brothers causing a racket. MAMMASANTISSIMA stands with her back to the audience at the top of the staircase made by adjoining ascending chairs. She waits for DON SASÀ to stand up and join her. The chairs bang out a pressing rhythm that serves as a rallying cry. DON SASÀ gets up and, following the noise, approaches to the throne. LIBORIO, scared, backs away, opening up stage right.

DON SASÀ:
May I come in?

The dogs stop moving the chairs.

I, Don Sasà, long to know, always please and thank you, who among you should I kiss?

The dogs climb the staircase to reach MAMMASANTISSIMA. *They kiss her on the mouth, and then climb down. After she has kissed everyone,* MAM- MASANTISSIMA *descends. The others kiss among themselves, always on the mouth.*

MAMMASANTISSIMA *gestures with her head to* BIG JIM *to kneel in front of* DON SASÀ *to set in motion The Rite of Recognition.*

DON SASÀ, *blindfolded, will have to pass the first trial: identifying* MAM- MASANTISSIMA. *He'll be able to touch with his hands the faces of whomever will kneel at his feet to be identified.* DON SASÀ *pushes away* BIG JIM *and* DAGGER *without hesitation. The same faith awaits* SLIM FAST *until* MAMMASANTISSIMA *decides to kneel down and face* DON SASÀ. *He takes off her hat and recognizes her immediately.*

MAMMASANTISSIMA *takes off* DON SASÀ's *blindfold, kisses him, and signs herself with the sign of the cross.*

MAMMASANTISSIMA:
In the name…

EVERYONE:
…of the Father, the Son, the Mother, and the Holy Spirit. Amen.

MAMMASANTISSIMA *undresses and prepares* DON SASÀ *for the second trial: The Lapidation.*

DON SASÀ (*to* MAMMASANTISSIMA):
Come, I'm waiting for you. I'm not scared. Come!

EVERYONE:
Go. Cut him open, kill him!

MAMMASANTISSIMA *lunges ferociously toward* DON SASÀ; *she hits him with her shoes, showers him with kicks, punches, and spit as she insults*

him without mercy. The others cheer her on and help her, ganging up on him.
Satisfied, MAMMASANTISSIMA *throws the suit she took off to the dogs;*
the same suit DON SASÀ *will wear.*
They help DON SASÀ *get dressed while he is still disoriented by the blows.*
As soon as the new affiliate is attired in his double-breasted suit, tie, and hat,
UNCLE TOTÓ *moves toward him to hug him while the others kneel in front*
of him. After festive hugs and kisses on the mouth, the dogs and MAMMA-
SANTISSIMA *cheerfully line up, tighten ranks, and walk back and forth*
reciting the "Our Mother" prayer while throwing stacks of money in the air as
if they were confetti.

Our Mother,
Who art on Earth
Hallowed be Thy throne
Thy Kingdom come
Thy will be done on Earth, in Heaven, and everywhere
Give us this day a bit of bread
And remit us our trespasses
As we remit to you those who trespass against us
And lead us not into temptation
But deliver us from the Father.

MAMMASANTISSIMA:
Offer each other a sign of peace.

The dogs punch each other and, right away, hug each other lovingly. They then
kneel, each in front of their icon, while DON SASÀ *recites The Oath.*

DON SASÀ:
I enter with blood
And I'll leave in blood.

173

Everyone rubs their holy card against their lips, smearing them with lipstick. Then they burn them using the flame of the candles.

I swear
To be faithful to my brothers
To never betray them
To help them always
And if I faulter
May I burn and be scattered
Like this image is scattered
As it is consumed to ashes.

The dogs blow on the ashes that disperse into the air. The plate stands become guns that the dogs point at each other's faces.

MAMMASANTISSIMA:
Whoever is not with me is against me!

MAMMASANTISSIMA *formulates the questions of The Ten Commandments of the Holy House.*

How many steps must we take to enter the Holy House?

EVERYONE:
Many.

MAMMASANTISSIMA:
He who doesn't kiss the feet of the Miraculous Virgin as he carries her in procession, how many teeth should be left in his mouth?

DAGGER:
Two.

MAMMASANTISSIMA:
He who wants to be a mother even before being a son, how should he sign himself?

JOKER:
Without hands.

MAMMASANTISSIMA:
He who slips inside a confessional to listen to that which only the Eternal Father should know, how shall we plug his ears?

GEGÈ:
With pieces of his own tongue.

MAMMASANTISSIMA:
He who can't see but still looks at what should not be seen, how shall we turn off his lights?

DON SASÀ:
We'll sew his eyes shut.

MAMMASANTISSIMA:
He who doesn't know where to put his feet because they point in different directions, how long shall he walk in circles before he can stop?

BIG JIM:
Until he, walking round and round, will have dug himself a grave.

MAMMASANTISSIMA:
He who doesn't go to bed when the cock crows, what should the bells sound before we put him to sleep?

MOUSE:
A funeral toll.

MAMMASANTISSIMA:
He who unnerves the woman of his brother, what shall we do with his dick?

SLIM FAST:
We'll split it and eat it.

MAMMASANTISSIMA:
He who turns the blood of his baptism into water, what can we do to make him die a decent soul?

UNCLE TOTÒ:
Drown him in his own blood.

MAMMASANTISSIMA:
He who sings and snitches, how many shots should we play in his mouth?

EVERYONE:
Do, re, mi, fa, sol, la, si.

MAMMASANTISSIMA:
He who doesn't swallow their pride when the brotherhood commands, deserves to be stabbed in the chest ten times.
And to enter the Holy House, one has to ask: "May I come in?"

The dogs slip the guns in their partner's mouth and, as couples, dance a waltz. PANUNZIO arranges the chairs with LIBORIO's help, positioning them from the shortest to the tallest around a long table. At the head of the table he places the throne where MAMMASANTISSIMA will sit. MAMMASANTISSIMA puts on a richly embroidered white skirt with a 14-foot long train that covers the table. Holding the train, the dogs festively accompany her toward the throne. When everyone is seated on their assigned chair in hierarchical order, the dogs lay down on their legs the table covered by MAMMASANTISSIMA's tablecloth/train. Scared, LIBORIO follows PANUNZIO and sits in front of him on the lowest chair.

The Rite of Bread and Wine begins. MAMMASANTISSIMA *hands the dogs a large bottle of wine and a piece of bread.*

Drink of it, all of you, for this is my blood.

The dogs take off their hats as a sign of respect. They place them on the table and, one by one, they drink the wine from the fiasco bottle that MAMMA-SANTISSIMA *has offered them.*

Eat of it, all of you, for this is my body.

The dogs/disciples rudely eat. They spit, they burp, they devour the bread with frenzied desire. MAMMASANTISSIMA *watches them, deep in thought.*

Slow down. You look like a bunch of market dogs. If you eat like that you'll choke and you'll get the tablecloth dirty.

UNCLE TOTÒ:
I'm full, Mammasantissima, because the honor to sit at your side, at this feast, is more filling than anything else.

MAMMASANTISSIMA:
Don Sasà!

DON SASÀ:
God bless you.

MAMMASANTISSIMA:
Do you still hear voices?

DON SASÀ:
Strong and clear.

MAMMASANTISSIMA:
Like your faith! You're a man of honor and you've earned this seat at my side, because you've done important things for me. Now, I ask you to do something important for my family.

DON SASÀ:
I'm entirely at your service, Mammasantissima.

MAMMASANTISSIMA:
Mouse, you look worn out. Are you sick?

MOUSE:
Women wear me out, Mammasantissima!

MAMMASANTISSIMA:
Yeah, women! Hookers, you mean!!

Everyone doubles over with laughter.

MAMMASANTISSIMA:
Gegè, how's the pharmacy going?

GEGÈ:
Pharmacies never go bankrupt.

MAMMASANTISSIMA:
Where there's life, there's illness!

They continue to laugh uncontrollably.

Big Jim we missed you, did you go on vacation?

BIG JIM:
In Sardinia, a real paradise on Earth.

MAMMASANTISSIMA:
Did you chop off the mustache, Slim Fast?

SLIM FAST:
I shaved it this morning and didn't even spill a drop of blood.

MAMMASANTISSIMA:
Dagger, how's school going?

DAGGER:
I'm working on my third degree, Mammasantissima.

MAMMASANTISSIMA:
Did you win at scratch offs yet, Joker?

JOKER:
I don't play anymore; I was going bankrupt!

MAMMASANTISSIMA:
You're so far away, Panunzio!

PANUNZIO:
Ready to stand up and follow your orders.

MAMMASANTISSIMA:
Down there, in front of you, there's a stranger.

Everyone looks at LIBORIO, who, embarrassed, puts on his hat and tries to make a joke.

LIBORIO:
What does a dwarf write on the wall?

Nobody answers but everyone continues to stare at him.

MAMMASANTISSIMA:
What does he write?

LIBORIO:
Down with cunts!

Nobody laughs. Everyone continues to stare at him and he, even more embarrassed, tries to explain the pun.

LIBORIO:
Down... he wants cunts to be lower, the little dwarf... so he can get to them. He is a dwarf... little... and he also has a right to those God-given marvels... (*Silence*) I know another one... Listen, listen up... breaking news: bomb at the cemetery. Everyone's dead! (*More silence*) It's a word game, shananigans. (*Pointing at* JOKER) You have to laugh! Since time immemorial when someone tells a joke the other one who's listening waits a bit and then he lightly grins... maybe if he liked it he even lets out a big laugh... (*Pointing at* DAGGER) You too have to laugh. I'd be happy even with a courtesy laugh... but why are you staring at me? What do you want? What...

DON SASÀ:
Liborio, calm down!

LIBORIO falls silent but shivers all-over. He takes off his hat and puts it back on the table.

I abided by Mammasantissima's wish to have a respectable person sit at our table.

PANUNZIO:
The Conductor Liborio Paglino.

MAMMASANTISSIMA:
This respectable person will be the most important guest.

BIG JIM *laughs wildly.*

(*She glares at him.*) There's nothing to laugh about!

BIG JIM *stops. Everyone is silent, while they wait for the word of* MAMMA-SANTISSIMA.

I took bread out of my own mouth so you could study! (*Pause*)
I paraded you around, speaking of you as if you were the best of the best.
Rising up and up, bit by bit you climbed to the top of this mountain…

MOUSE:
And during the climb, we never got afraid.

BIG JIM:
For you, Mammasantissima, we wore off our feet and knees.

MAMMASANTISSIMA:
You conquered the place you were due and no one better touch it!

SLIM FAST:
No one!

The dogs look at LIBORO.

MAMMASANTISSIMA:
You're now ready to descend, my sons! The biggest is ready to become the smallest. The smartest becomes the dumbest and who's in charge is ready to serve.

BIG JIM:
What am I hearing, Mammasantissima?

MAMMASANTISSIMA:
Do what I tell you: make your way down, scooting over one by one until Don Sasà and Uncle Totò find themselves at my feet on the last chairs in place of Liborio the Railway Man and Panunzio the Doorman.

Nobody moves.

(*Screaming*) Panunzio!

PANUNZIO *jumps to his feet and invites the others to quickly climb down from the chairs. Everyone is dumbfounded but they don't dare disobey her.* DON SASÀ *and* UNCLE TOTÒ *sit on the shorter chairs where* LIBORIO *and* PANUNZIO *sat before. The others remain standing.*

Don Sasà, place your gun on the table. Uncle Totò, you do the same.

The two take the guns out of their pockets and lay them on the table.

Who's in charge?

In a flash, UNCLE TOTÒ *points his gun at* DON SASÀ *who stands still. Silence.*

Don Sasà, this way you'll lose!

DON SASÀ:
You've never pointed a weapon at me, Mammasantissima, and yet I've always respected your commands. Without saying a word!

MAMMASANTISSIMA:
Because I could explain myself and I never felt the need to raise my voice or to shoot to reiterate my commands. Isn't that right, Uncle Totò?

UNCLE TOTÒ:
Quite right!

MAMMASANTISSIMA:
Then: disarm! All of you! (*To everyone*) Take out your guns and hide them under the table, because I don't want to see them anymore. Quickly.

The dogs follow the order. They disarm, placing the weapons underneath the table.

Attention! Don Sasà, this baby chair is now yours and, at my side, in the seat you've conquered for yourself with so much effort, I'll put an ordinary person: Mr. Railway Man Liborio Paglino. What do you say to that?

DON SASÀ:
I ask for the reason.

MAMMASANTISSIMA:
And if I told you this was fair, would you trust me?

DON SASÀ (*after a thoughtful pause*):
Certainly, Mammasantissima.

MAMMASANTISSIMA:
Uncle Totò, what's your answer?

UNCLE TOTÒ:
The same.

MAMMASANTISSIMA:
Well done! How satisfying it is to reason with you all! Panunzio, once again I've been able to explain myself, and you, who are the last among my servants, have gotten a nice promotion: sit at my side, up here, come on! The same honor goes to you, Liborio Paglino. The Doorman on the right, the Railway Man on the left, in the two seats of honor. (*To the others*) The rest of you, line up those chairs with the appropriate marks that I've got to make a speech. Seriously! And open your ears!

The dogs push the chairs away from the table and open them up like a fan, placing each of them in front of an arrow. The five chairs on one side mirror the five on the other. DON SASÀ and UNCLE TOTÒ sit in the lower seats assigned them by MAMMASANTISSIMA, while LIBORIO and PANUN-ZIO climb to the sides of the throne, taking the seats that were previously occupied by DON SASÀ and UNCLE TOTÒ.

Take a seat everyone!

Everyone sits in their usual place, ignoring MAMMASANTISSIMA's wish.

Are you comfortable?

JOKER:
Very, Mammasantissima!

MAMMASANTISSIMA:
Ah no, Joker! I think that if you sit next to Don Sasà, you'll be more comfortable!

After a moment of hesitation, JOKER *moves down one seat.*

Mouse, come up here beside Panunzio.

MOUSE, *euphoric, climbs up one seat.*

Dagger, where would you like to sit?

DAGGER (*pointing at* GEGÈ's *chair*):
Here!

MAMMASANTISSIMA:
Granted: Gegè, get down!

Speechless, GEGÈ *stands up.* DAGGER, *quick as lightening, takes his place.*

Slim Fast, talk to Uncle Totò a bit, he's feeling lonely, poor man; Gegè, there's an empty seat left; Big Jim, sit down!

BIG JIM:
But this is Slim Fast's seat. Mine is this one! (*Pointing at the chair where* MOUSE *is currently sitting*). It's higher!

MAMMASANTISSIMA:
That's your younger brother's seat now.

BIG JIM:
Mammasantissima, I've been in and out of jail my whole life, I've never ratted out anyone and Panunzio can vouch for me, I've always kept quiet so I could be next to you and now you want to send me away?

MAMMASANTISSIMA:
I'll feel you close to me just the same. You shouldn't get attached to material things in life. (*To LIBORIO*) So dramatic!

BIG JIM:
Mammasantissima, you taught Mouse how to behave and he, like the civilized person he is, should've asked my permission before sitting on my chair! (*To MOUSE*) Come on, get down and ask for permission!

MOUSE is about to get down.

MAMMASANTISSIMA:
I gave him permission.

MOUSE:
I'm nobody, Mammasantissima! I can't sit above Big Jim. I didn't do any-thing to deserve it! It's not fair!

MAMMASANTISSIMA:
Life isn't fair! Big Jim, show your brother how one gets big and take a seat in the chair I assigned you!

BIG JIM hesitates for a moment and then moves toward the shorter chair MAMMASANTISSIMA had pointed out to him .

BIG JIM:
Gegè!

GEGÈ:
Ah!

BIG JIM:
Are you comfortable?

GEGÈ:
No.

BIG JIM:
How come?

GEGÈ:
This isn't my chair!

BIG JIM:
So?

GEGÈ (*to* MAMMASANTISSIMA, *working up the courage*):
I worked my ass off with the Colombians, the Afghans, the Nigerians, and the Filipino, bringing in cocaine, heroin, crack, kobret, and shàboo. I sweated to get that fucking chair and what do you do? You give it to that piece of shit of a man who's never done a damn thing in his whole life?

DAGGER:
How dare you, you animal? You're still stuck on cocaine while I busted my ass to make you win government contracts and subcontracts.

GEGÈ:
Dagger, get down from there you ass-clown!

DAGGER:
Did you forget about the single span bridge?

BIG JIM:
But if we haven't even broken ground yet, Dagger! It's a bridge to Messina and money should've come to us! That was the deal, wasn't it?

DAGGER:
It's not my fault the government changed: we were almost there!

BIG JIM:
It's 30 years that we've been waiting for this blessed bridge on the strait, Dagger, stop dumping on our dicks!

DAGGER:
Should I get down and rip both your asses? I'm coming down!

GEGÈ:
Come on pretty, get down!

MAMMASANTISSIMA:
Don't you move from that fucking chair!

SLIM FAST:
Mammasantissima is right, Dagger earned that chair, by constantly plastering walls with giant copies of his face and putting his hands on documents and official records, he made the family rich. Not like us, who are still stuck in the Stone Age. Do you do drugs, Gegè?

GEGÈ:
Me? As If I would ever! I'm a good boy.

SLIM FAST:
Me too... I'm someone who works, not someone who jerks people around!
Dagger, now that you've started your rise to power, why don't you go peck around Autonomia Siciliana St., Tukory Avenue, and Maqueda St. the whole damn day under the blazing sun?

DAGGER:

Are you all still dealing with bribes? Goodbye racket! You don't need to
peck around all day under the blazing sun anymore, Slim Fast. By now,
we are the economy. Instead of asking businessmen for a percentage on
their earnings, we should lend them money and when they can't give it
back because the interest rate is too high, their businesses become ours!
Now, Slim Fast, answer me this: if their businesses become ours, who are
we going to charge for protection money? Ourselves?

SLIM FAST:

Big Jim! Dagger asked me a question… a difficult one… and I'm trying
hard to answer him, but trying so hard's making me wanna take a dump!

SLIM FAST stands up and pulls down his pants. Everyone, including
MAMMASANTISSIMA, laughs hysterically.

Joker, aren't you sitting in Dagger's chair?

JOKER:
Se.[33]

SLIM FAST:
And you feel nothing up your ass?

JOKER:
As a matter of fact, I also sense the urge coming since I feel like I'm sitting
on a throne.

JOKER pulls down his pants. He runs around with SLIM FAST as they
pretend to hold in a dump.

SLIM FAST:
Uncle Totò, where's the toilet?

UNCLE TOTÒ
I'm constipated.

SLIM FAST:
And I'm gonna shit myself. Ahhh! I've got an idea. Mouse, lend me your hat, thank you! (He steals MOUSE's hat.) Joker, swipe Dagger's hat?

JOKER:
Great idea!

SLIM FAST and JOKER snatch MOUSE's and DAGGER's hats, then they exchange places. SLIM FAST moves toward JOKER's chair, near DON SASÀ, and JOKER takes over SLIM FAST's chair. SLIM FAST shows JOKER what to do. He puts the hat upside-down on the chair.

SLIM FAST:
Follow my lead, Joker: ease the hat down on the chair, then grab your underwear. Mammasantissima, may we? ...One... two... and...

JOKER:
Three!

They both pull down their underwear, sit on the hats, and take a shit with utmost satisfaction.

SLIM FAST:
These are the pleasures in life, Don Sasà!

MAMMASANTISSIMA:
The smell is killing me! Joker, when was the last time you changed your underwear?

JOKER:
Mammasantissima, today of all days I put on clean underwear for the occasion.

MAMMASANTISSIMA:
Slim Fast, all done?

SLIM FAST:
All done.

MAMMASANTISSIMA:
And so, why don't you make Dagger eat your shit like you did with that child before you shot him in the mouth?

Silence. SLIM FAST *stands up and slowly pulls up his underwear. He looks at her from below.*

SLIM FAST:
Mammasantissima, I never mix work with play. This useless thing is my brother, blood of my blood, and I could never disrespect him like that.

MAMMASANTISSIMA (*to* JOKER *and* SLIM FAST):
Then, since you're moved by such brotherly feelings, you'll give the hats you have on your heads to your brothers, and you lot shall put on the ones that were under your asses.

SLIM FAST *and* JOKER *carry out the order, then they go sit in their places.*

Big Jim, Gegè, instead of standing there upright like the pricks you are, go sit down in the seats Mammasantissima assigned to you!

GEGÈ goes to sit down but BIG JIM doesn't move.

What are you waiting for, a court order?

Everyone laughs, except BIG JIM.

BIG JIM:
Mammasantissima, first I'd like to ask Dagger, who, by now, has become an expert on the 'new economy,' how come he made us lose, in addition to the bridge project – with government contracts and subcontracts already assigned –, the bid for that waste-to-energy plant that we'd asked him to keep an eye on? That was money, never mind the bribes!

UNCLE TOTÒ:
You can only talk trash, can't you Big Jim?

BIG JIM:
But why, Uncle Totò? Are landfill management and chemical waste recycling trash or business to you?

UNCLE TOTÒ:
This question's out of line: Dagger has nothing to do with it and you, with this talk, are offending me and only me, because you know that it's my jurisdiction to remove trash! So, get out of my face, Big Jim, and go sit down. You should trust more. We're working for you.

BIG JIM:
What working and working, Uncle Totò, you haven't done anything, you scored a bundle of votes and our thanks was the 41-bis.

SLIM FAST, GEGÈ, *and* JOKER *stand up.*

UNCLE TOTÒ (*to* SLIM FAST):
And therefore, I didn't do anything! That's what I have to hear from a deadbeat who, every time he goes on vacation, leaves the whole family to deal with it while he freeloads!

BIG JIM:
But why, do I go on vacation for myself?

GEGÈ:
Go sit down, Big Jim!

UNCLE TOTÒ:
Gegè, answer me: do you feel ok?

GEGÈ:
I'm ok, thank the Virgin!

UNCLE TOTÒ:
I'm ok too! Everyone here enjoys excellent health, don't they? We have the best private hospitals in Europe, where the best among the best specialists work, all luminaries; ambulatories, diagnostic centers, laboratories of nuclear medicine that are the topmost in the world and everyone can suck it; we've got the health system that brings us money! And all this seems little to Big Jim?! Gegè, it's so true that when you toss pearls before swine you just get splattered with shit…

BIG JIM *applauds and engages the others in a standing ovation for* UNCLE TOTÒ. *Everyone congratulates* UNCLE TOTÒ *for the beautiful speech and* UNCLE TOTÒ, *with the intention to make peace, approaches* BIG JIM.

(*To* BIG JIM) Take off your hat, Big Jim.

BIG JIM *takes off his hat.* UNCLE TOTÒ *head-butts him unexpectedly with such violence that* BIG JIM *collapses to the ground precisely on top of the painted body outline.*

Scum of the Earth!

BIG JIM *gets back up, stumbling, and pounces on* UNCLE TOTÒ. *The others block him, trying to calm him down.*

JOKER (*pulling his shoulder*):
You need to calm down!

BIG JIM:
And you shouldn't touch me... (*He punches* JOKER.) Touch me again, and I'll slaughter you! (*To* MOUSE) Mouse, go sit in the chair that Mammasantissima gave you!

After taking the punch, JOKER *falls on the body outline but stands up almost immediately to go after* BIG JIM. GEGÈ *stops him.*

GEGÈ (*to* JOKER):
Calm down, nothing happened.

JOKER (*to* BIG JIM):
Big Jim, I always spoke well of you!

GEGÈ:
Joker, shut up, calm down!

JOKER (*to* GEGÈ):
I'm calm... I'm calm. (*To* DAGGER) Dagger, bring me my hat on all four!

DAGGER:
What am I, a dog?

JOKER:
Yes.

MAMMASANTISSIMA:
Joker, go sit down.

GEGÈ:
Dagger, that chair doesn't represent you

DAGGER:
And you, sir, what do you represent? A fucking prick?

MAMMASANTISSIMA:
Shut up or I'll slaughter you!

JOKER:
Dagger, I swear on the Holy Mother: bring me the hat or I'll rip off your head and stomp on it!

DAGGER:
And I'll sue you!

GEGÈ:
What did you say?

DAGGER:
I'll sue you!

JOKER (*ironically*):
Then I gotta look for a lawyer!

SLIM FAST:
Dagger, do you know a good one?

MAMMASANTISSIMA:
Go sit, I said; down!

JOKER:
...then I'll bring that cashmere hat back to Dagger...

GEGÈ:
...he's a real fine man!

SLIM FAST (*to DAGGER, screaming*):
Get off that fucking chair!!

*SLIM FAST grabs DAGGER by the hair and throws him on the ground
JOKER kicks him and then wipes his feet on DAGGER's hat. A vicious brawl
breaks out during which the dogs overturn the chairs in front of MAMMA-
SANTISSIMA in sign of protest.
DON SASÀ doesn't take part in the revolt; on the contrary, as a sign of
devotion to MAMMASANTISSIMA, he sits on the ground at her feet,
ignoring the fight. DON SASÀ's striking gesture breaks off the commotion.
The dogs direct their attention toward DON SASÀ.*

DON SASÀ:
For me it's enough to sit on the ground before you Mammasantissima,
and I won't lose my dignity. Even better! What we are, we carry it on our
shoulders and we never lose it.

MAMMASANTISSIMA:
Did you get it? Unworthy, criminals... you should sit at my feet! On the
ground, you crooks! Because I am your God. Thieves! Blasphemers! If I
climb down, I'll set your insides on fire and knock down heaven with all
its saints!
Stand up, Don Sasà!

DON SASÀ:
I can't get up by myself, I've got sciatica!

MAMMASANTISSIMA:
Big Jim, help him!

BIG JIM slowly heads toward DON SASÀ and helps him get up.

DON SASÀ (*to BIG JIM*):
Thank you. Thank you very much! May God repay you! Uncle Totò and I
are sitting on the lowest chairs but that doesn't mean that we don't count
for anything!
(*To LIBORIO*) How're you doing up there, Liborio? Do you see what
confusion you've brought? Mammasantissima, may I make up for it and
put some order in this chaos?

MAMMASANTISSIMA:
That's why you're here, Don Sasà.

DON SASÀ:
Liborio, am I less important than you?

LIBORIO:
No!

DON SASÀ:
Then why are you sitting in my seat?

*LIBORIO feels all eyes on him. Scared, he looks around, but he sees every-
thing out of focus because of the glasses. He calms down only when he locks
eyes with MAMMASANTISSIMA, who seems to be smiling at him.*

LIBORIO (*pointing at* MAMMASANTISSIMA):
The lady told me to!

DON SASÀ (*to* LIBORIO):
Right! You've carried out orders and you've done well.
(*To the dogs*) He also has a dignity of sorts, he's good, loyal, and gets attached quickly. (*To* LIBORIO) Is it true or not?

LIBORIO:
Yes.

DON SASÀ:
And we, what have we done, Uncle Totò? To take care of our business we've neglected him, leaving him alone! Do we want to honor his presence per Mammasantissima's wishes, or don't we? What do you think, Slim Fast?

SLIM FAST:
That in here a guest is sacred, especially if he's a friend of yours.

DON SASÀ:
Libò, would you explain to everyone why you've become my best friend?

LIBORIO:
Because you've helped me find a job.

DON SASÀ:
I know how to help my friends, it's true, and my friends know that when Don Sasà asks, they have to give. What would you be willing to do for me, Libò?

LIBORIO:
Everything.

DON SASÀ:
Everything, everything?

LIBORIO:
Without any problem whatsoever.

DON SASÀ:
A moment ago, Slim Fast made a gesture near my chair I didn't much
care for. Would you explain to him that certain needs are to be relieved in
the crapper?

*DON SASÀ stares at SLIM FAST while he moves closer to LIBORIO who
begins to shiver.*

(*To* LIBORIO) Give him a slap for me.

LIBORIO (*shaking his head to say no*):
It was nothing… a joke… he'll understand it on his own…

DON SASÀ:
Libò, it's a favor I'm asking.

*After a long silence, LIBORIO is about to get down from the chair but, since it
is too tall and he risks breaking his neck, he pulls back. He takes off his glasses
and once again tries to climb down. He makes it. He moves toward SLIM
FAST very slowly while everyone watches him. Now he sees them well, the
dogs. Their faces are mean. Their mouths, hungry. He looks for DON SASÀ's
eyes and finds them. He directs a pleading look toward him. DON SASÀ
encourages him to take the last steps toward SLIM FAST who is waiting for
him, arms crossed. With his head down and his hands sweaty, LIBORIO
freezes in front of SLIM FAST. Then, lightning fast, gives him a hard pat on
the cheek and runs to hide under a chair.
Everyone nearly dies laughing.*

I'd like to know who learned you how to slap people! Didn't you see that that, to Slim Fast, didn't do a thing?

DON SASÀ *heads decisively toward* SLIM FAST *and plants a huge slap square in his face, making his hat fly off. Laughter subsides. Speechless, everyone looks at* DON SASÀ.

(*Laughing*) That's a slap!
Libò, pick up the hat for Slim Fast, otherwise he'll start crying... ha, ha, ha!!!

LIBORIO *starts moving toward the hat but he's stopped in his tracks by* DON SASÀ.

On all fours!

SLIM FAST *understands* DON SASÀ*'s intentions and relaxes.* LIBORIO, *terrified, carries out the order getting on all fours. Everyone laughs at him.* DON SASÀ *hugs* SLIM FAST *who puts on the hat* LIBORIO *brought him.*

(*To* SLIM FAST) See how good he is? I'm very proud of him. (*To the dogs*) That's why I gave him my seat. What did you think, that I'd give it to anyone? (*To* LIBORIO) Liborio, do you know what it means to be in charge?

LIBORIO:
No.

DON SASÀ (*pointing at his chair*):
But who sits up there has to call the shots.

LIBORIO:
I could stand though, I'm used to it.

MAMMASANTISSIMA (*standing up*):
If he stands, then I have to stand too.
Liborio, my children are here to celebrate you: ask and you shall receive.

DON SASÀ:
She's asking you to make a wish, take advantage of it!

LIBORIO:
I don't need anything, thank you!

DON SASÀ (*whispering*):
What are you doing? You can't refuse; it would be too big of an insult against Mammasantissima. Go on, be brave, what would you like?

LIBORIO:
I... I would like to leave.

DON SASÀ:
That's your wish? Then you're an ungrateful man! Why, we let you sit at our table, I gave you my seat, you saw and heard about our things... you understand that you can't leave the same way you came in. First, we have to play hangman! Would you like to participate?

LIBORIO:
I don't know how to play.

DON SASÀ:
It's really easy, listen to me: the guest, to participate, must have a sin to confess. If the guest has sinned, then we can play.
Mammasantissima thinks of a word that she hides within a full sentence and we have to guess it.

LIBORIO:
And what should I do?

DON SASÀ:
If we guess the word right, you must be the hangman!

The dogs almost die laughing.

JOKER:
Go on, confess!

LIBORIO:
I don't have any sins!

JOKER:
Come on… everyone has sinned a little!

LIBORIO:
I swear in front of God!

PANUNZIO:
Vibo Valenzia Pizzo Station, does that ring a bell?

LIBORIO:
You swore you wouldn't tell.

DON SASÀ:
He's right, Panunzio. He has to tell it! Come on, Liborio, it's another favor I ask of you.

Silence. LIBORIO is trapped. He can't escape. He puts his glasses back on and, in a whisper, recounts the accident of which he is tragically responsible.

LIBORIO
Vibo Valenzia Pizzo Station, time: 23:42, I put on my glasses through which I see nothing… I pull out the lantern to give the "Ready to Go" signal… the doors close… the driver turns on the engine… and…

He can't go on. He stops.

PANUNZIO:
…and the train… sets off!

PANUNZIO smacks LIBORIO whose hat flies off.

Paglino! What did you do? (*Pointing at the hat that fell on the ground*) The head of your young colleague, the conductor on duty… decapitated!

LIBORIO takes off his glasses and looks at DON SASÀ. Then he works up the courage and runs to get back his hat. PANUNZIO gets there first, grabs the hat, and, excited, throws it to the dogs, making them take part in this cruel game.

The head rolls… rolls… rolls…

UNCLE TOTÒ:
From Track 3…

MOUSE:
To Track 2…

JOKER:
To Track 1…

GEGÈ:
How disgusting! A dead man's head!

BIG JIM:
Catch it, Liborio.

SLIM FAST:
Grab the head, Libò…

The dogs, circling around LIBORIO, *throw the hat at each other, mimicking the bouncing of the severed head.* LIBORIO *tries to grab it but he falls. He stands back up. He loses his glasses. He gets injured.* PANUNZIO *puts his own hat on* LIBORIO'*s head and the railway man crosses himself. Then, exhausted, he falls to the ground in front of* MAMMASANTISSIMA, *in the same spot where* DON SASÀ *sat earlier. With a wide-brimmed hat on his head and his back to the audience,* LIBORIO *looks like one of them.*

MAMMASANTISSIMA (*to* LIBORIO):
Put your glasses back on and don't repent for what you've done, because it is not a sin. You have no faults. The poor are always right, even when they're in the wrong. Come to me!

LIBORIO *stands up. As he moves toward* MAMMASANTISSIMA, *he notices his hat on the ground and bends down to pick it up. He takes off Panunzio's hat from his head and brings it back to him on all fours.*

(*To* LIBORIO) Don't crawl on all fours; you're a respectable person Liborio and you've been an example for us all.

MAMMASANTISSIMA *addresses the dogs, calling them by their name, thus revealing their identity.*

Thank you, Cardinal Salvatore Spagniuolo, you did something important for my family, showing everyone that, to rule, guns are of no use; nor it is useful to sit at my side, (*pointing at the throne*) because this seat, by now, is worth nothing.

You too are a respectable person, Governor Totò Siciliano and there's no need to conceal your name because no-one can do you harm, no-one should be afraid anymore, you mustn't hide your names, all of you must become respectable people, because I do not exist.

Trust me. We still have a ways to go, but you'll climb down from this mountaintop and reach the valley where you'll entrust my conscience onto everyone.

The country will be ours! You'll rest your asses on seats of power: right, left, center – what does it matter where you'll sit? I'll be your shadow and I'll follow you everywhere. You don't have to content yourselves anymore with the crumbs on the tablecloth because the real feast is underneath it.

Believe me: I don't exist.

And it's right for journalists to write that on your newspaper, Gennaro Panzanella. Tony Cintola, the bridge will be built, don't worry. Undersecretary Giuseppe Bonanno, you'll open construction sites for major public infrastructures all over the country. Water is the business of the future, more so than drugs, doctor Girolamo Riccio. Vito Montalto, Stefano Varvarà: continue to defend the values of the family even if it costs you your lives but do blend in with ordinary people and don't show yourselves anymore wearing those trashy clothes: throw everything away! Colonel Federico Panunzio: help your brothers in their time of need.

With my consent: may God bless you.

In the name of the Father, the Son, and the Holy Spirit. So Be It.

The dogs throw their hats in the air. They help MAMMASANTSSIMA *lift the train/tablecloth to uncover the table. A gigantic map appears, depicting an upside-down and divided Italy. Sicily is in the North. The dogs, downstage, hide their faces behind transparent masks and start to undress.* MAMMASANTISSIMA *descends from her throne, her face covered by a black veil. With a brush, she writes syllables on each of the dog's backs,*

starting with LIBORIO. *On* LIBORIO's *back she writes "*IO.*" As each indi-
vidual receives his letters, he turns toward the map of Italy hanging from the
upstage grid, pulls down his underwear, and begins to masturbate. When
everyone has turned their backs toward the audience, a sentence appears:
"*IO-MA-DRE-VI-AF-FI-DO-L'ITA-LI-A.*"[34] *Excited, the dogs read the
syllables written on their backs. They ejaculate while the map flies up and a
noose with an attached counterweight descends.* MAMMASANTISSIMA
slides the noose around LIBORIO's *neck. The counterweight presses on his
face. The dogs fall to the ground to reveal the word thought up by* MAMMA-
SANTISSIMA. *Only three of them remain standing. On their backs is spelled
the word: "*MA-FI-A.*"*

MAMMASANTISSIMA *unties the counterweight and* LIBORIO *dies
hanging.*

The Eyeglasses Trilogy

◆

Holywater

The Zisa Castle

Dancers

Three Studies on Characters, not Plot

The Eyeglasses Trilogy focuses on three issues of marginality – poverty, illness, and old age – but it is love that ultimately links together the relationships between characters. Everyone puts on eyeglasses. They are half-blind, melancholy, and alienated. They blow their nose and drool. They perspire sweat and tears. Because they love. Madly. Each with their own intimate music: a music box for the old lovers, a megaphone playing the refrain from *Titanic* for the nostalgic sailor, and the lullaby of the little dolls-princesses that spin round and round in front of a sleeping Nicola. There is no plot in *The Eyeglasses Trilogy*, like there isn't in life. Three human and inhuman conditions merrily tell of their suffering.

Speflector is on the bow in front of the sea, his face splashed by the spurts of the waves as he watches tropical fish… the coral reef… a harlequin octopus with multicolored tentacles… and a jellyfish… gigantic… entangled in the rays of the sun… the sea that changes color every minute… and the pufferfish that inside itself holds the future and the past… and the Christ of Rio that swan dives from the tip of the Corcovado… and an iceberg… enormous… that melts into crystal tears inside the depths of the sea…

He listens to the ticking of the heavens above his head. Then everything falls silent. The sea stops breathing and Speflector feels his heart skip a beat: one day the ship sailed without him leaving him mad and alone on the dock of a foreign country: *terra firma*. He, of all people, who has devoted his life to sailing, who feels lost if he doesn't sway, who by day and by night needs to behold his one great love: the sea. The voices of the crew, the captain, echo in his head and the cabin boy becomes wood as he waits for the ship to return, like the figurehead of an old galleon.

A fall from a chair unleashes the unbridled running of Nicola who drools and oozes out sweat after having been huddled up and forgotten for far too long. His eyes are open but he doesn't see. Two women clean him up, feed him, scold him. He has been curled up on a small chair since

209

he was removed from his house in the Zisa quarter. He used to spend all day at the window looking at a marvelous castle... with a dragon mask and clawed gloves, he shooed away the devils perched on the tower to defend the princesses... but one day Nicola is deposed and he becomes spellbound, forever. His childhood, his lightheartedness are locked in the Zisa Castle... We are the ones who see him stand up after the fall, lift his eyes to the sky, let out a scream trapped in the body, we are the ones who hear him speak, laugh, light up with passion. The refrain of two little twirling mechanical dolls carries us back inside the dream.

The old dancer pulls out of the trunks the memories of her life. Among them is the most beautiful one: her husband; it's New Year's Eve but she can't celebrate alone. She calls her groom, pulls him toward her with the melody of an old music box. Tall and skinny, he emerges from a trunk and heads toward her, a tiny and bent over figure. Out of habit, she's always at his right side and when they are near each other, the pronoun *it* comes to mind. He pulls out a watch from his breast pocket and counts barely moving his lips: 5... 4... 3... 2... as midnight tolls, he sets off a small firecracker and festively throws a handful of confetti in the air. She looks at him. He looks at her. *it* dances. He, with his chin resting on her head. She, holding on to his jacket. *it* draws closer and they kiss as they did their first time.

The Eyeglasses Trilogy is dedicated to our grandparents and their memories, which render loneliness poetic; to loved ones who fell ill and left smiling, without as much as a whimper; to the beggars who we encounter every day on the streets and don't feel like listening to.

— EMMA DANTE

Holywater

◆

A beggar's thoughts in italics

"You know a thousand things, a thousand you uncover
that are hidden to a simple shepherd.
Often, when I watch you
keep so silent on a desert plane
bordering the sky in its furthest circle;
or follow me with my flock,
journeying little by little;
and when I look at the stars burning in the heavens;
I think to myself:
— Why so many flames?
what makes the air infinite, and that profound
infinity, serene? what does this immense
loneliness mean? and what am I? —"[35]

— GIACOMO LEOPARDI
from "Night Song of a Wandering Shepherd in Asia"

CHARACTERS:

SPEFLECTOR

Who also plays:

THE CAPTAIN

and

THE SAILOR

I'm kneeling before this rusty bow, tied to three anchors hanging from the light-ing grid. The anchor attached to my right ankle weighs 5 pounds, the one tied to my left ankle 7.5 pounds, and the central one, tied to the back of my belt, weighs 11 pounds. Mostly, it's the 11 pounds on my back that get to me, by the end of the day I can't move from the pain. I found them in the sea, that's why all three are encrusted in seaweed and shells. From the grid, I hung five upside-down bottles that slowly drip water. Underneath the bottles, five bowls collect the drops. I like the sound of water; it makes me feel at home.

People come in, they take their seats in front of me. They're all here for me! They lower their eyes pretending nothing is happening, but I know they see me. I look at them intensely, my eyes pleading. Each of us plays our part. I've put a small plate in front of the bow with a sign that reads "Thank you." I comb my hair trying to straighten up the part on the left, once in a while I drink from a plastic bottle that I always keep handy, I wipe the corners of my mouth with the handkerchief I keep in my pants' pocket.

My corduroys are worn, my t-shirt is faded, my shoes have holes, with the corner of my eye I check to see if the plate is still empty, I drink again, I spray water through my teeth toward the outside of the bow to water the stage, I comb my hair, I blow a whistle tied to a little chain around my neck. They call me SPEFLECTOR *because of my specs. The reflection off my lenses in which others see themselves.*

As soon as everyone has taken their seat and the doors of the theatre close, I turn on the lights that illuminate the inside of the bow with a mischievous smirk on my face. I built it myself this bow, with two metal sheets I found at the little Acquasanta[36] *harbor. I drink again and I stand up, water in my mouth. Above my head I hung thirty or so kitchen timers that I rush to set by stretching upward while balancing on my toes. Tick tock tick tock tick tock… I set them for 40 minutes. Tick tock tick tock tick tock… in the meanwhile I gargle… gargle gargle gargle gargle… The engines ignite…tick tock tick tock… I move the lines to which the anchors are attached and, as they begin to oscillate, I also sway from one foot to the other… I swing until the sea becomes rough… it becomes rougher and rougher… the waves crash against the side*

of the ship... I stagger... lose balance... slip... I grab on to the anchors... the sea is force ten.
I blow the whistle with all the strength I can muster. There's a terrible storm... And they just sit there, arms folded and moronic expressions on their faces! I grab the hat of THE CAPTAIN *who's screaming like a madman.*

THE CAPTAIN:
All hands on deeeck! Tighten the sheets! Getoffofthere you fool - it's dangerous! We gotta take it astern otherwise we'll capsize!

I take advantage of a moment when he's distracted to lean out on the rail and dive into the sea. I swim, trying to counter the tides, I barely stay afloat... a whirlpool pulls me down... I'm happy... mad with happiness. THE SAILOR *sees me, bastard, he always has an eye on me... He sounds the alarm. I put on his cap.*

THE SAILOR:
Maaan overboooard!

I reach the ship with difficulty and, after various attempts, I get back on board cold and shivering. I return to the bow and I pick up a small megaphone into which THE SAILOR *screams.*

THE SAILOR:
Speflector report to the Captain! I repeat, Speflector report to the Captain immediately.

I'm excited. I tuck my T-shirt inside my pants, I take off the cap, and I speak to the audience, which hasn't moved, not even an inch.

218

SPEFLECTOR:
Sweet Mother of God I hate this sailor! His eyes are always on me. I've got him here, breathin' down my neck. He thinks the Captain's callin' me 'cause he's gonna punish me but the Captain likes me an' instead he'll for sure want to reward me for my heroic behavior during the most dangerous sea storm that ever was.

I put THE SAILOR's cap back on.

THE SAILOR:
I repeat, Speflector report to the Captain immediately.

I stand at attention in front of THE CAPTAIN.

SPEFLECTOR:
I really can't stand this piece of shit sailor! There's the Captain, how handsome! Yessir, Captain, sir!

I take off the cap and the glasses, I let the line tied to my left foot pull me over and I listen to my Captain. I put on THE CAPTAIN's hat.

THE CAPTAIN:
But what have you done Speflector, did you jump overboard again?

I take off the hat, put on my glasses, straighten my T-shirt.

SPEFLECTOR:
I didn't jump, Captain, I fell. Just ask 'em!

I turn to the audience.

They're all witnesses here, that storm was like being inside a Tsunami, inside that ride, what's it called, the Tagadá. Nobody could understand anything anymore... them too they were all twisted up, flyin' purses, kids rollin' around, seniors hangin' in the balance.

I put THE CAPTAIN's *hat back on.*

THE CAPTAIN:
That's not true, I saw you leaning on the rail when we were coming about.

The hat comes off, I defend myself.

SPEFLECTOR:
I was counterbalancing, Captain, if it wasn't for me, we'd have capsized! I took hold of the reins of navigation, with my own strength I kept the ship steady.

A fat lady in the audience looks at me tenderly.

Ma'am, you see me all skin and bones but when things like these happen, I turn into Superman...

THE SAILOR *chimes in, putting his cap back on my head.*

THE SAILOR:
Don't believe him. We all saw him - swan-diving into a force ten sea!

He can't always have the last word… I get rid of the cap.

SPEFLECTOR:
My glasses were flying off and trying to catch 'em I fell in too! Ya' know these specs are my brains. (*To the fat lady*) They call me Speflector, Ma'am, 'cause of the lenses, they reflect things back, but I don't get offended, these lenses are the representation of my intelligence, I keep it constipated inside my brain, my intelligence, otherwise it explodes. You too, over there (*to an old man in the middle of the audience whose eyelids close from time to time*), with the glasses, isn't it true that if you take 'em off all of your intelligence explodes?

THE SAILOR meddles once more.

THE SAILOR:
Instead of saying bullshit, why don't you clean your mouth? You'll make us greet out guts.

How embarrassing! I quickly take a handkerchief out of my pocket and clean the corners of my mouth. I can't control my saliva when I speak, I'm sorry.

SPEFLECTOR:
This is sea-foam. It's not disgusting to me. Do you think it's disgusting, Ma'am? No, in all honesty… the lady seems a little disgusted, but come on, don't be like that, this is sea-foam… ok ok, Ma'am, if you're going to leave, then I'll wipe it off.

I clean myself with the handkerchief but the saliva reappears at the corners of my mouth.

You see, there it is again. I take it off… an' it comes back… off an' back… I can't do anything 'bout it, it's an unfair fight, like wanting to drain the sea. But seeing as the sea has never done anything to me, every time there's danger I'm the first to dive in. And now, for all these rescues I did for them, they should put up a statue of me like Garibaldi's or Cavour's.

I strike a pose.

I want it like this the statue, the pride of navigation. No, I'll lose my balance like that. Like this: me lookin' at the anchor…

THE SAILOR *pulls the line tied to my right foot.*

THE SAILOR:
But when have you ever saved anyone, Speflector, the one man overboard has always and only been you!

He's so unworthy, I don't even glance at him.

SPEFLECTOR:
And every time I fell, I've saved myself.

THE CAPTAIN *pulls the line tied to my left foot.*

THE CAPTAIN:
This farce has got to end: you throwing yourself overboard, we tossing you a lifesaver, the ship that has to stop... we're here on board to earn some money, it's not like we're on a cruise on the Love Boat!

THE SAILOR interrupts.

THE SAILOR:
Why don't we leave him at sea next time, Captain? Since he only wastes our time, this grand idiot!

THE CAPTAIN raises his voice.

THE CAPTAIN:
Silence. Everyone, back to your posts - we've got to resume navigation. Set course toward Rotterdam.

THE CAPTAIN leans down toward me and speaks softly.

THE CAPTAIN:
Speflector, you've got to get your head in order because next time I won't be able to defend you anymore! Go on, get to work!

I go back to the bow, feeling proud. THE CAPTAIN defends me, he likes me, he understands me. I look at the sea, inhaling deeply. I turn on the megaphone and I stretch outward, holding on to the lines. It's that song from Titanic.

SPEFLECTOR:
I want it like this, the statue, on the bow, like the figureheads of ancient galleons.

I sway following the rolling of the ship.

So many things I've seen from this ship... so many! The sun and the moon, one in front of the other throwing rays of light at each other, knotting 'em and making 'em go down, straight down into the sea... I've seen the sea change its color... and a swordfish with two swords... and a gigantic jelly fish entangled in the rays of the sun and the moon... and a pufferfish that within itself held the future and the past... and from the top of this bow, I've dived into a coral reef where each coral was the statue of a saint in paradise... and I've seen a harlequin octopus with tentacles of every color and tropical fish dancing above and below them... and the Christ of Rio, I've seen him plunging headlong from the Corcovado into a swan dive... We swam a few laps together and then we started somersaulting in the water with the Statue of Liberty, her boobs all hanging out... she was top-less... I've held on to the fin of a barracuda that brought me to the other side of the world... Japan... where there were fish with almond eyes eating other fish, raw... like sushi... and I've seen a galleon from three centuries ago, full of people who were dancing and singing songs from times past... and an iceberg... enormous... melting into crystal tears inside the depths of the sea.

I fall silent. It hurts to remember happiness when there's sorrow in one's heart. I'm sad, very sad... I turn off the music and confidentially speak to the audience.

I did everything on that ship, since I was fifteen. I worked in the machine room, I cleaned the toilets, I peeled potatoes, I made breakfast, croissants and brioches, I cleaned the deck, the bulkheads, I sanded, painted, tied

knots then untied them and then tied them again just so I could learn, I
made lunch and dinner first and second shift, I'd eat too on the fly if I had
five minutes 'cause I first had to serve the officers and petty officers, and
then I cleared the tables, washed the dishes, cleaned the toilets again and
at night, when I'd finished my work, before going to bed, I'd go to
the stern, underneath the starry sky, to watch the shapes the propeller's
foam made in the water… and I'd be overcome by 'a 'ppocundria…[37]
longing… I saw mom's face, my buddies from Brunelleschi avenue, those
delicious taralli made with lard and pepper from 'o Granatiello…[38] and
I'd feel like throwing up.
So I'd look in front of me and to stop thinking about it, I'd start singing.

*I take off my glasses and look into infinity. The retching becomes more
insistent.*

"Ohè! Chi sente e chi mo' canta appriesso a me… ohè, pe' tramente s'af-
faccia 'a luna pe' vedè" (*I put on my glasses, puke a little in the handkerchief*)
"pe' tutta 'sta marina da Procida a Resina se dice guarda là 'na femmena
che fa…" (*the retching slowly disappears*) "Maruzzella Maruzzè t'hai miso
dint'all'uocchie 'o mare e m'hai miso in petto a me 'nu dispiacere… 'stu core
me fai sbattere cchiù forte 'e l'onde quanno 'o cielo è scuro… primma me
dice sì, poi doce doce me fai murì… Maruzzella Maruzzè…"[39]

*I sing the refrain at the top of my lungs, I even dance a little and my face lights
up.*

One day I discovered that the best place to face the sea is here, on the
bow, toward becoming.

I'm looking at the horizon… but I only see the darkness of the theatre.

I don't have a home, a family, a friend, I don't even have a change of clothes, I don't know what it means to satisfy a whim, to have fun, I've always only worked, always. To give an example: the deck – long twenty-eight of my steps and usually getting cleaned in half an hour – took me, took me an hour and fifteen minutes to clean, 'cause I'm meticulous; I'd polish it to a mirror finish: when I could part my hair using my reflection on the deck, only then I'd be satisfied! I taught this handful of boat people how to do everything, these castaways, these bums, these processed industrial by-products: routes, winds, naval terminology, all the stars in the sky, one by one, I taught 'em, about knots, and currents… without me they wouldn't even float… 'cause the half cabin boy is the most important role in all of marine navigation.

I sing at the top of my lungs.

"Maruzzella Maruzzè t'hai miso dint'all'uocchie 'o mare e m'hai miso in petto a me 'nu dispiacere… 'stu core me fai sbattere cchiù forte 'e l'onde quanno 'o cielo è scuro… primma me dice sì, poi doce doce me fai murì… Maruzzella Maruzzè…"[40]

THE SAILOR snaps his fingers and pulls my right foot.

THE SAILOR:
Just drop dead, Speflector. Do you get it or not? You're useless on this ship!

I look at him with hatred.

SPEFLECTOR:
That's not true! Without me you'd all go under!

I run to the bow, I turn the megaphone back on, I take control of the wheel and I veer northwest. Watch this beautiful come about, you ugly piece of shit!

I've done the math, to get to Rotterdam we have to head northwest, it's a shortcut!

THE CAPTAIN becomes suspicious.

THE CAPTAIN:
What's happening? This isn't the direction on the route!

Worried, THE SAILOR looks around with a hand on his balls.

THE SAILOR:
Affirmative Captain, my compass is never wrong, we're not heading northeast, we're heading northwest.

THE CAPTAIN realizes they're in danger.

THE CAPTAIN:
We're on a collision course; we're going to head straight for the rocks!

THE SAILOR rushes to the bow, pushes me aside, grabs the wheel and comes about left. I resist and reset the course to the right.

SPEFLECTOR:
No, you gotta trust me, I did the math!

THE SAILOR tears the wheel from my hands.

THE SAILOR:
Speflector, take your hands off this wheel - we're heading straight for the rocks!

I try to reason with him while I keep the wheel steady.

SPEFLECTOR:
And so what? This ship is indestructible, if we hit a rock, the rock will disintegrate! That's my shortcut, we're gonna do a piece of it by land!

THE SAILOR, exasperated, retakes possession of the wheel.

THE SAILOR:
By land? What land, you dickjacket?

I hit him with a karate move and I take over as helmsman again. The bastard bites my wrist and, proud, cap on his head, steers the ship northeast once more. I tickle him. He can't resist and laughs.

No, no tickling.

I answer, clarifying.

SPEFLECTOR:
Oh yes tickling, tickling is allowed!

THE SAILOR *gets really angry and snatches the wheel away from me once and for all.*

THE SAILOR:
Speflè, if you don't take your hands off this wheel, I'll call the Captain and I'll have you dismissed!

I let go.

SPEFLECTOR:
Let's not say anything to the Captain!

THE SAILOR *looks at me disdainfully.*

THE SAILOR:
Let's not say anything, how? You were about to sink us!

Me? How can he say such a thing?

SPEFLECTOR:
Even so? We're fully stocked with life rafts, they're brand new, we've never used 'em!

THE SAILOR *cracks a sarcastic smile.*

THE SAILOR:
You lost your mind, Speflector. You've become dangerous. We're going to the Captain!

He grabs my arm, jerking it.

SPEFLECTOR:
Ouch, ouch, you're hurting me! No, not to the Captain, if he makes me get off this ship it's the same as killing me! Let's not say anything to anyone, let's make it a secret between you and I.

THE SAILOR looks at me, dead serious.

THE SAILOR:
And what are you gonna give me in return?

Me? What can I give him? I don't have anything. Nothing at all…

SPEFLECTOR:
Ouch, ouch! Not my hand, please, not my hand…

THE SAILOR lowers his pants and puts my hand inside his underwear.

THE SAILOR:
Like this, Speflector… slowly, slowly… don't worry, we won't say anything to anyone.

I jerk off that revolting scum… slow tempo, long strokes… he likes it like this… that become shorter, and shorter… up to the tip… fast fast… and… filthy, disgusting worm… after he ejaculates, he hangs me upside-down by the feet.

SPEFLECTOR:
Whoa! Whoa! What the fuck are you doing? Don't drop me… don't drop me! Hey, what the fuck are you doing? Blood's going to my head like this. Let me down! Someone let me down! I need air, I can't breathe! Capta-aain! Call the Captain!

The coward unties my feet… I fall hitting my head.

You have to stop it with these pranks. What's this bullshit here – putting my feet up in the air and my head in the water? People die like this. I was drowning. Like that other time when you left me outside the entire night. I got bronchitis and had to stay in bed for three days. Why do you always pick on me? What did I ever do to you all? You steal my cigarettes, take my mineral water, hide my toilet paper, put glue in my shoes… Enough is enough… now I'm not afraid of your threats anymore: I'm going to the Captain and I'll rat you out one by one… this way he'll dismiss you all and it'll finally be only he and I on this ship. Now you've really pissed me off! Come on, let's go! One at the time, face to face…

The bastard hangs me upside-down again. I can't breathe like this… I can't take it…

Whoa! Whoa! Mama, maaama! I need to breathe, I need air…mama! I can't breathe anymore…

I convulse. I'm going to suffocate if no one unties these lines.
The wretch sets me free and pulls his pants up while he splits his sides
laughing.

THE SAILOR:
I'd like to know why the Captain insists on keeping you on this ship,
when he could replace you with a Filipino and pay him half of what he
pays you.

I take the handkerchief out of my pocket and clean the hand that jerked
him off.

SPEFLECTOR:
What does a Filipino know about navigating big ships? He's used to going
from island to island with a canoe, a paddle. Does a Filipino know knots
the way I know 'em? What does a Filipino know of a hitch knot, a half
hitch, a single Savoy knot, slipped and/or in series, a Franciscan knot,
multifold overhand knot, a monkey's fist, a flag-man's knot, sheet bend,
reef, English, granny, bowline, Portuguese bowline, Spanish bowline, tri-
ple bowline, sheepshank, buntline hitch and slipped buntline hitch, taut-
line hitch, slipped anchor bend, cleat wind, angler's loop, slip knot... The
Filipino wouldn't even know how to tie his shoes... because he doesn't
have shoes...he wears flip flops!

THE SAILOR laughs.

THE SAILOR:
You're too funny, Speflector, real entertainment. When we get to Rotterdam you'll get off with us, we'll go have some fun, we'll take you to the
red district and you'll show us if you're a man.

I answer him as usual.

SPEFLECTOR:
You know I don't get off. I don't believe in these things.

THE SAILOR pulls my left ear.

THE SAILOR:
Then it's true you're all… heeeyyy…. Heeeyyy…!

We laugh.

SPEFLECTOR:
What are you thinking? I don't believe in solid land!

I look at THE SAILOR. I'm serious once again.

It's an illusion; it's inside your heads. I've seen the mistake you make.
When the ship leaves the dock, you all get on deck at the stern: "Bye,
mamà, don't cry, don't worry - I'm already on my way back… sweetheart,
make sure not to bring anyone home with you 'cause if I find out something happened, I'll come back and I'll kill you…papa's princess, study
hard, do your homework, and don't piss off your mamà because when
daddy comes back he'll bring you a nice present!" I don't say goodbye to
anyone, have you ever seen me say goodbye to anyone? Who am I going
to say bye to? I don't have anyone. That's what gives me the chance to see
things you can't even imagine, when the ship leaves the docks, I see the
lights gettin' smaller and smaller and the harbor, the piazza, the city move

away. I see the distance. But the most important thing is that the world, bit by bit, goes away… it detaches itself… What's the world? It's nothing! That's why I didn't want to get off this ship anymore; it's a sentimental matter. 'Cause I fell in love. I got engaged to infinity.

THE SAILOR, hands on his balls, moves his pelvis back and forth.

THE SAILOR:
And did you fuck it, Speflector?

He makes me laugh with his pantomime of fucking.

SPEFLECTOR:
Does it seem possible that I could fuck the sea?

On the bow, I brace myself against the lines and I stretch out toward the sea.

The sea is impalpable, immense, pure. The sea is my girlfriend! I look into her eyes, only a few meters away. Whoosh! Whoosh! What are you doin', sea? Sending my way the splashes of your waves? Quit it! You're giving me a bath! Stop! I've gotta tell you somethin' important and this time everyone has to hear it. Everyone has gotta hear it. It mustn't be a secret anymore, I can't keep it inside any longer. Whoosh! Whoosh! Eh eh eh! Stop! Whoosh whoosh! All right, give me a bath! After all, for me, this is blessed water. It's holywater! From the first moment I saw you, I couldn't understand anything anymore. I didn't know day from night… I only thought of you, I wanted to be alone with you…

THE SAILOR makes fun of me.

THE SAILOR:
Speflector, so you're really fuckin' the sea?

I ignore him.

SPEFLECTOR:
Don't listen to 'em, they're kids, they only think about that dirty stuff. But I, since I met you, I don't think about all that filth anymore. Sea, I love you.

THE SAILOR is jealous of me…he doesn't have a love as big as mine. That's why he turns everyone against me and even tries it with THE CAPTAIN. He gets worked up, he calls him…

THE SAILOR:
Call the Captain, he has to come see this he too has to come see this, Speflector is declarin' his love for the sea. He went and gone crazy!

Yes, I'm crazy, yes…

SPEFLECTOR:
I'm crazy for you, sea!

THE CAPTAIN will understand. He'll defend me. There he is!

THE CAPTAIN:
What's happening here? Why aren't you all at your stations? The ship is drifting!

He won't listen to THE SAILOR, *no, he won't…*

THE SAILOR:
Captain, they're all witnesses here, Speflector lost his mind, that's why he doesn't do anythin' anymore and we've gotta finish all his duties. Tear him off that bow and make him get off this ship otherwise there's going to be a mutiny!

THE CAPTAIN *comes close to me and speaks softly.*

THE CAPTAIN:
I can't defend you anymore, Speflector, there's too much tension up here, go, take a leave!

I give THE CAPTAIN *a kiss, I give it to him on his forehead, because I also care about him.*

SPEFLECTOR:
But where am I gonna go, Captain? The sea is my whole life!

THE SAILOR *comes to the bow, takes the megaphone and shouts.*

THE SAILOR:
We can't stand him anymore, either he leaves or all of us will. Cesspit! Dirty rag! Will you leave or not? Captain, confine him!

I slowly put the megaphone back in its place. I look at the anchors behind me and feel discomfort from the lines tied to my ankles and my back. I move backward. I now hear very loudly the water drops falling from the ceiling. I still have THE SAILOR's *cap on my head, but I can't make him talk anymore... How strange... I find myself imitating him with mechanically disconnected gestures, with disarticulated movements. I take off the cap and I try with* THE CAPTAIN's *hat. Same thing. I stop. I try again to move* THE SAILOR, *then* THE CAPTAIN, *the whole machinery is stuck, they don't respond anymore. I stop, I feel discomfort in my back, the anchors are incredibly heavy, with difficulty I slowly move forward, I reach the bow and look at the sea, at infinity.*

SPEFLECTOR:
Sooner or later they'll be back. They'll go around the world and then they'll come back here! They can't leave me here. All my stuff's on the ship! I don't have anythin' here...

I take off my glasses and grab on to the lines, leaning forward on the tip of my toes. I sing.

"Tramonta 'a luna... e nuje, pe' recità l'urtima scena, restammo mane e mane, senza tenè 'o curaggio 'e ce guardà... Famme chello che vuò... indifferentemente, tanto 'o ssaccio che sò: pe' te non sò cchiù niente! E damme 'sto veleno, nun aspettà dimmane... indifferentemente... si tu m'accide nun te dico niente."[41]

I put my glasses back on, do a little dance, then, still holding on to the lines, I open up my arms like a figurehead ready to challenge the ocean.

The Zisa Castle

◆

The fall inside the dream

"Nothing has changed.
Except perhaps the manners, ceremonies, dances.
The gesture of the hands shielding the head
has nonetheless remained the same.
The body writhes, jerks and tugs,
falls to the ground when shoved, pulls up its knees,
bruises, swells, drools and bleeds.
Nothing has changed.
Except the run of rivers,
the shape of forests, shores, deserts and glaciers.
The little soul roams among those landscapes,
disappears, returns, draws near, moves away,
evasive and a stranger to itself,
now sure, now uncertain of its own existence,
whereas the body is and is and is
and has nowhere to go."[42]

— WISLAWA SZYMBORSKA
from "Tortures"
in *View With A Grain Of Sand*

CHARACTERS:

YOUNG NUN

OLD NUN

NICOLA

A room in a religious institution for the care of the sick. Four chairs lean against the back wall, each covered with a white sheet. Above each chair dangles a small white crucifix. Two women kneel in silent prayer in front of the chairs while glancing sporadically toward the crosses. Both women, one young the other older, wear slips. Their hair is down, their feet are bare. They finish praying, stand up, kiss the crucifix, cross themselves and move toward a corner of the room where their carefully folded clothes are lying on the ground. The women pull up their hair into tight buns and get dressed in semi-darkness, whispering among themselves.

YOUNG (*She puts on her glasses.*):
Did you mend Nicola's pajamas?

OLD:
Weren't you going to do it? Je l'ai fait l'année dernière... (*She also puts on glasses.*) You, instead: did you iron the sheets?

YOUNG:
I did many other things... (*She puts on a white shirt and quickly buttons it up.*) I dusted the toys... swept the floors... cleaned the bathrooms... made breakfast... washed the dolls' tiny dresses... look!

The young woman points to two mechanical dolls dressed like princesses located a few meters away.

OLD:
But what do you care about the dress if that doll hasn't worked in years! It spins so slowly, it's exasperating! (*She puts on a black skirt and a white shirt.*) Don't tell me you cleaned and straightened up parce que c'est pas

245

vrai! C'est tout en désordre! Tu dis vraiment n'importe quoi! You just say crap!

YOUNG (*She also puts on a black skirt.*):
If you speak French, I don't understand a fucking thing!

OLD:
Depuis tout ce temps you should have learned French.

YOUNG:
I don't understand what you're saying, moron!

OLD:
All right now... (*She takes off her glasses.*) Mettons les points sur les i...
Listen carefully...

YOUNG (*She takes off her glasses and gets closer to the older woman's face.*):
No, you listen...

OLD:
Hulà! Mais tu t'es pas lavé les dents, c'est une infection!

YOUNG:
Nicola's pajamas need to be mended and the toys organized...Who's going to do it?

OLD:
What do you mean who's going to do it? Yesterday, I did it, today, it's your turn.

YOUNG:
Mine? Then you're hard of hearing! This morning, I did more than I had to, therefore you'll do the rest! Do you understand my language? Unbelievable!

OLD:

Quoi? Ah non mais alors là vraiment c'est le ponpon!

YOUNG:

Go do your duty, go!

The young woman puts on a pair of flats and, arms crossed, waits for the other woman to move.

OLD:

Tu es mesquine! Vraiment mesquine! Like I didn't fulfill my duty. Like I didn't do anything at all, all day. Je me casse le dos toute la journée à nettoyer, à cuisiner, à repasser, à ranger, j'ai pas une minute pour moi... jamais! Je suis extenuée... je suis éreintée... destroyed. Va te faire voir!

After putting on a pair of black flats, the older woman moves toward the chairs grumbling and stomping her feet. From under the sheets she pulls out a few bowling pins, a hula hoop, and small, colorful balls, which she arranges at the feet of the chairs. When she returns, the young woman has put on a black apron and the white veil worn by catholic nuns.

OLD:

See, it took me two minutes... when you do it, it takes you half an hour because instead of thinking about order, tu fais la maline avec l'hula hoop...

YOUNG:

I experiment with new exercises... on myself... so when it's time to do them with the patients it's easier, I know how... here, hurry up!

She hands her an apron and a veil.

OLD (*quickly putting on her nun garments*):
J'expérimente des nouveaux exercises. Tu es la plus malade, ici! And I am the one who slaves away all day!

YOUNG:
You're not proactive… never… I've read a multitude of books… I go to the cinema when I can… to the theatre… I watch TV… I experiment continuously.

OLD:
Et on voit le résultat! Bravà!

The YOUNGER NUN *picks up a large leather bag and wears it cross body. They both move toward the first chair in the row. They bend over to grab two corners of the sheet and, as if it were the most natural thing in the world, they uncover a young man curled up on the chair, his upper torso folded forward. Like the other patients covered by sheets, the young man doesn't show signs of life.*
In this room of the institution, they are all soundly asleep. The OLDER NUN *lifts up* NICOLA, *and brusquely takes off the shirt of his pajamas.*
NICOLA's *eyes are wide open but he doesn't see. He lets the women handle him like a rag doll. The* YOUNGER NUN *takes two tissues from her bag and hands one to the sister. They spit on the tissues, lift up* NICOLA's *arms and rub the tissues against his armpits. After lowering his pants, they repeat the same action between his buttocks and genital area.*

OLD:
Nicolà regarde-moi! Toujours le même! Tu es paresseux. Lazy! Leve le bras, ouvre la main, tourne la tête… allez un petit effort. A little effort, come on!

YOUNG:
Hurry up, pull down his underwear. I don't have time for this!

OLD:
Hulà! Il transpire… Il sent mauvais!

YOUNG:
Wipe his ass instead of complaining. Here's another tissue.

OLD:
You wipe it while I go wind up the dolls…

She moves away to wind up the princesses that, as they spin, generate a tune.

YOUNG (*loudly, to* NICOLA):
If she wasn't here to take care of you, you'd piss and shit all over your-self… let's wait for her together, ok? Poor devil…

The OLDER NUN *comes back and angrily sticks a tissue between* NICOLA's *buttocks.*

OLD:
Allez maintenant on va te nettoyer les fesses… let's clean up your cheeks. Hulà! Il a fait caca!

She hands the dirty tissue to the other sister.

YOUNG:
But why are the most disgusting things always up to me? My Lord let this torment end soon!

OLD (*looking at* NICOLA's *penis*):
Hulà! Il a un gros zizi! Tous mes compliments, Nicolà!

The YOUNGER NUN *throws the shit-stained tissue in a corner of the room, then she bends down and picks something up. When she reappears, she is wearing a dragon mask. She plants herself in front of* NICOLA *and, emitting frightening noises, she mimes the monster's movements.*

OLD:
Qu'est-ce que tu fais avec cette maskerà?

YOUNG:
What kind of question is that? You see me do this pantomime everyday... I do it to startle him, to make him react!

OLD:
But if you see that it doesn't work, why do you insist?

YOUNG:
Because I believe in miracles.

The OLDER NUN *snatches the mask and starts to move toward the doll that in the meanwhile has stopped spinning.*

OLD:
Espèce d'arrogante!

The YOUNG NUN *whispers incomprehensible words in* NICOLA's *ear and, meanwhile, throws him a ball, puts the hula hoop around his arm giving it a spin to make it rotate, plays with three balls in front of his face hoping that his eyes will move... react... but nothing, nothing happens... the boy does not respond to any stimulus, his pupils are dilated, his eyes dead. The* OLDER NUN *returns and, after turning his head toward one of the two carillon-dolls,*

she feeds him with a spoon full of mush taken from a little jar. The YOUNG
NUN *takes a comb out of the leather bag and begins to comb his hair.*

OLD:
Does this seem like the right time to comb his hair?

YOUNG:
Sooner or later you'll poison him with that concoction.

OLD:
Tell me honestly: what would you like me to feed him?

YOUNG:
What did you put in that?

OLD:
Carrot puree and tomato sauce.

YOUNG:
That's disgusting! Aren't you ashamed of feeding him that?

OLD:
Why don't you make him something to eat then?

As the OLDER NUN *quickly turns toward the sister, she bumps* NICOLA's
shoulder. He falls from the chair.

YOUNG:
Moron, you've made him fall!

OLD:
I made him fall, huh?! Qu'est-ce qu'il faut pas entendre?!

The OLDER NUN *bends over* NICOLA, *pulls him up and sits him back down. Then she abruptly turns around and once again hits* NICOLA's *shoulder. He falls down in the same position as before.*

YOUNG:
You see? You're the one who makes him fall. You didn't put him back in the chair correctly! You're incompetent!

OLD:
I didn't put him back correctly! Qu'est-ce qu'il faut pas que j'entende de la bouche d'une gamine! You go break your back! You pick him up and you put him back! Go on! Do it!

YOUNG:
What? You made him fall and I have to pick him up? Are you completely stupid?

OLD:
I'm stupid, huh? You don't even help me, do you realize that? You like it when he falls… so you can throw it back in my face! You don't feel pity for him… for anyone! How will God forgive you?!

YOUNG:
You know what? I'm not doing anything else today. You deal with it!

OLD:
Ça changera pas grand chose, since you've never done anything.

YOUNG:
Don't you dare talk to me like that, you understand? Now I'm going for real and then we'll see if nothing changes!

OLD:

Viens ici! Alors, let's speak clearly and let's start from the beginning: how do you expect me to feed him while you're combing his hair? Can you explain that to me?

YOUNG:

I can't collaborate with you…there's no listening. You're deaf. You can never feel when it's the right moment to do things.

OLD:

Ah, I can never feel when it's the right moment to do things?!

YOUNG:

I can't stand you anymore. If you keep on provoking me, I'll explode! Look at the doll, her dress is coming apart, look at Nicola, his pajamas have holes, the food you give the patients is disgusting, the toys are broken, the sheets stained…

OLD:

Shut up a moment - I don't understand. Tu parles en permanence, c'est insupportable! I can't get anywhere with you… To go on like this c'est pas possible! Je deviens folle! I'll have a nervous breakdown. Je suis exaspéré, tu me ruines l'existence, tu comprends?!

YOUNG:

I'm at the point of no return, not you! I'm exasperated! I beg you, dear Lord, stop me because I'm about to commit a homicide.

OLD:

Oui, voyons! Do it! Tue-moi! Kill me if you have the courage! Je suis là. J'attends…

The YOUNGER NUN repeatedly kicks the sister with unbelievable ferocity.

253

Arrête! Arrête! Je t'en prie! Pour l'amour de Dieu, arrête! Tu me fais mal, tellement mal! Ce n'est pas possible de continuer comme ça, je n'en peux plus, moi! Je suis arrivée au bout, à la limite du supportable. J'ai des bleus énormes sus l'arrière train, des bleus grands comme ça! Je me passe de la crème tous les soirs avant d'aller au lit mais rien n'y fait! J'ai l'arrière train tout gonflé. Je souffre, moi! Tu te rends compte de ce que tu me fais subir depuis des années? On ne peut pas continuer comme ça, non, ça n'est pas possible! Le matin, quand je me lève, je suis pliée en deux, tellement je souffre, comme ça! Je fais en effort surhumain pour me redresser. J'ai du mal à marcher, non mais tu te rends compte? Oh mon Dieu, je vous en prie, faites quelque chose pour moi! Aidez cette pauvre femme à retrouver la raison, elle est folle, c'est une folle! Je vous en supplie mon Dieu, aidez-moi à surmonter cette épreuve! Je veux bien souffrir comme le Christ sur la croix mais aidez-moi...[43]

The YOUNGER NUN, *her face distraught, kneels down and prays under her breath.*

YOUNG:
Lord, forgive me...

The OLDER NUN, *crying, lies on the floor flat on her belly and, in stretching out her arms like a cross, she hits one of the two dolls. The doll tips over and stops playing. While the two women are absorbed in prayer,* NICOLA *gets up from the floor and sits on the chair. When the* OLDER NUN *pulls herself up,* NICOLA *falls to the ground once more in the same position as before. The two nuns, distressed, turn toward him.*

YOUNG:
Did you see him too?

OLD:
Bien sûr!

YOUNG:
He pulled himself up and fell down. My God!

Carefully, the OLDER NUN *goes closer to* NICOLA *while the other follows her, visibly frightened.*

OLD:
Help me! Let's pull him up!

The two women put NICOLA *in the chair and, after having observed him, the* YOUNG NUN *puts the hula hoop around his arm and gives it a spin.* NICOLA *responds to the spin giving the hoop enough momentum to complete two, three, or four revolutions.*

YOUNG:
Good Nicola! Good! Like this… keep going, don't stop… Yesss… Make it spin, Nicola… Make it spin… Faster… Go on!

OLD:
Vite, vite Nicolà! Et voilà! Maintenant let's try with the ball. Catch it! (*She tosses him the ball and* NICOLA *catches it*) Bravò Nicolà, like this… bravò!

Ecstatic, the two nuns continue to throw him balls, big and small, and bowling pins until NICOLA *wakes up from his lethargy, his body jerking. He cries out in pain. He stands up from the chair, takes two steps, and falls. The* YOUNG NUN *helps him to get on his feet.* NICOLA *takes four steps and falls. The two nuns exhort him to stay on his feet.* NICOLA *falls down and stands up several*

*times until he manages to stay upright, placing one foot behind the other as if
he were learning to walk again.*

YOUNG:
Hold on tight to the balls, Nicola, and walk, good, like that, you won't
fall, see?

OLD (*She throws three small balls in the air.*):
Regarde Nicola! Fais-le toi aussi, lance les boules et rattrappe-les, comme
ça, regarde! You do it too, throw the balls and catch them, like this, look!

NICOLA *throws the balls in the air and catches them like a real juggler
would.*

Bravò, bravò Nicolà!

NICOLA *lets the balls fall and leaps forward doing cartwheels, somersaults,
and backward tumbles. He runs… sprints around the room… wild with
happiness… but as soon as he glimpses the gaze of the audience, he comes to a
halt downstage. He looks at them, his head leaning right and left until he loses
his balance and falls. The* OLDER NUN *brings him a pair of glasses. Once he
puts them on,* NICOLA *sees better and regains his balance. He wiggles and
giggles, staring at the audience in astonishment. In a sudden fit of euphoria,
he fidgets until he is overcome by retching spasms; he then stares mesmer-
ized at the doll that the* OLDER NUN *had tipped over during her prayer.
The* OLDER NUN *runs toward the doll and, as soon as she pulls it upright,*
NICOLA *breaks out of the spell.*

NICOLA (*Curious, he talks to the two nuns and the audience.*):
My name's Nicola. I'm from Palermo, from the Zisa.

I spend the whole day in front of the window lookin' at the Zisa Castle. I am the guardian of the castle.

I live with my aunt Marisa, she loves me, my aunt! In the mornin' she calls me: "Get up Nicola!" No, aunty, I'm sleepy. "Get up - the milk's ready!" I get there run runnin' 'cause me, I like milk, it makes me stronger, but not just one cup! Me, I drink five, six cups... a river of milk... we've got a faucet for water and a faucet for milk, 'cause there's a cow on the roof with little tubes stuck to her teats, pressurized: peeeew peeew! It's a little much, this imagination I got! Milk's good for everythin': you scrape yourself and make yourself milk compresses, you break your wrist and you soak it in a milk bath, you get a headache, you take two milk drops, and if aunt Marisa gives me a slap... does it turn red? I put milk on it and it turns white... you got to rub it, though! Rub it!

NICOLA slaps himself repeatedly, the glasses fly off his face. The two nuns try to calm him down but the fit escalates. He hits himself hard, hurting himself, so the YOUNG NUN runs to wind up one of the dolls in an attempt to grab his attention.

YOUNG:
Nicola, look... look! It's music... the princess spins and plays music!

Captivated by the music box, NICOLA calms down and stares, spellbound, at the princess until she stops moving... then, calm and smiling, he focuses his attention on his pajamas.

NICOLA:
They are full of holes, my pjs! They're all ripped up! They're dirty, look! When I get dirty my aunt Marisa gives me a first-rate bath. She washes my head, hair, ears, armpits, belly button, balls and asshole! (*He mischievously looks at the nuns.*) She washes my balls and my asshole... and my

pee pee… one must always wash the pee pee otherwise it gets inflamed and it swells up! It swells up as big as this room!

He slides his hand inside his underwear and touches his penis.
He ejaculates prematurely. The YOUNGER NUN *cleans his hand with a*
tissue and, preceded by the other nun, begins to move upstage.

All clean and smellin' nice, my aunt puts me in front of the window and goes to work, she works at the hardware store… "Don't open the door for anyone, Nicola!" Nooo, aunty! I'll stay here, lookin' at the Zisa Castle… it's tall! I can't see where it ends! It has a tower where two princesses hide… They're very pretty! Dainty! The devils would like to snatch them, but I defend them! My window's full of eyes and claws… and my mouth breaths out air all day long, once in a while a devil passes by and I suck him in!

He runs to get the dragon mask, puts it on, and returns downstage making
dreadful noises accompanied by ample and disjointed gestures. Then he takes
off the mask and lifts his gaze toward the tower of the castle.

I scared off all the devils! I ate the smaller ones!
One night my aunt came back and brought me bolts… she gets them from the hardware store, the bolts… I make a lot of contraptions with bolts… that night for her I made a dragon with wings, I made! "Nicola, are you hungry?" Se…[44] "Should I make pasta with potatoes for you, the one you like?" Jeee, is it Sunday?! "Sit down, Nicola. I have to talk to you!" One minute, come here aunty, look outside the window! Look how beautiful the castle is… it touches the moon… it turns into silver with all those tiny stars framing it like a crown!
What are those black spots, aunty? It's full of dark spots up there! It's the devils perched on top of the tower! The princesses are in danger! "Sit down Nicola - I have to tell you something important!" What is it, aunty?

"You can't stay with me anymore." Why? "I can't have you here anymore."
But I wanna stay with you, aunty. "It can't be helped, Nicola!" Then you
come with me, aunty! "I can't come with you, but I'll come visit once in
a while." (NICOLA *cries*.) In the name of the son of the holy spirit! "No,
Nicola, in the name of the father, the son, and the holy spirit." I'm the
guardian of the castle! I'll defend you, aunty! The devils can't do anythin'
to us 'cause I'll eat them, I'll eat them horns, tails, wings and everything!
Their iron hoofs too! In fact, iron doesn't do anythin' to me. Iron makes
me even stronger! One time, a devil kicked me, aunty, and I ate his foot.
He walked away lame. Another time a devil kicked me twice and I ate his
feet, he walked away on his hands, like this… (*He turns to look at the nuns
who are waiting for him near the empty chair.*) In the name of the son of
the holy spirit! "No, Nicola… in the name of the father, the son, and the
holy spirit." The devils made me get it wrong, aunty! It's not my fault! In
the name of the son of the holy spirit! In the name of the son of the holy
spirit! "In the name of the father, the son, and the holy spirit!" Help me
aunty! In the name of the son of the holy spirit! In the name of the son of
the holy spirit! "No Nicola… in the name of the father, the son, and the
holy spirit!" You're tickling me like that, aunty! In the name of the son of
the holy spirit… help me aunty!

NICOLA *crosses himself as he moves backward toward the chair. A sudden
blackout interrupts the action. When the lights turn back on,* NICOLA *is on
the floor in the same position as before.*

YOUNG:
You see? You're the one who makes him fall. You didn't put him back in
the chair correctly! You're incompetent!

OLD:
I didn't put him back correctly! Qu'est-ce qu'il faut pas que j'entende de
la bouche d'une gamine! You go break your back! You pick him up and
you put him back! Go on! Do it!

YOUNG:

What? You made him fall and I have to pick him up? Are you completely stupid?

OLD:

I'm stupid, huh? You don't even help me, do you realize that? You like it when he falls… so you can throw it back in my face! You don't feel pity for him… for anyone! How will God forgive you?!

YOUNG:

You know what? I'm not doing anything else today. You deal with it!

OLD:

Ça changera pas grand chose, since you've never done anything.

YOUNG:

Don't you dare talk to me like that, you understand? Now I'm going for real and then we'll see if nothing changes!

OLD:

Viens ici! Alors, let's speak clearly and let's start from the beginning: how do you expect me to feed him while you're combing his hair? Can you explain that to me?

YOUNG:

I can't collaborate with you anymore…there's no listening. You're deaf. You can never feel when it's the right moment to do things.

OLD:

Ah, I can never feel when it's the right moment to do things?!

YOUNG:

I can't stand you anymore. If you keep on provoking me, I'll explode! Look at the doll, her dress is coming apart, look at Nicola, his pajamas have holes… the food you give the patients is disgusting… the toys are broken… the sheets stained…

OLD:

Shut up a moment - I don't understand. Tu parles en permanence, c'est insupportable! I can't get anywhere with you… To go on like this c'est pas possible! Je deviens folle! I'll have a nervous breakdown. Je suis exaspéré, tu me ruines l'existence, tu comprends?!

YOUNG:

I'm at the point of no return, not you! I'm exasperated! I beg you, dear Lord, stop me because I'm about to commit a homicide.

OLD:

Oui, voyons! Do it! Tue-moi! Kill me if you have the courage! Je suis là. J'attends…

The YOUNGER NUN repeatedly kicks the sister with unbelievable ferocity.

Arrête! Arrête! Je t'en prie! Pour l'amour de Dieu, arrête! Tu me fais mal, tellement mal! Ce n'est pas possible de continuer comme ça, je n'en peux plus, moi! Je suis arrivée au bout, à la limite du supportable. J'ai des bleus énormes sus l'arrière train, des bleus grands comme ça! Je me passe de la crème tous les soirs avant d'aller au lit mais rien n'y fait! J'ai l'arrière train tout gonflé. Je souffre, moi! Tu te rends compte de ce que tu me fais subir depuis des années? On ne peut pas continuer comme ça, non, ça n'est pas possible! Le matin, quand je me lève, je suis pliée en deux, tellement je souffre, comme ça! Je fais en effort surhumain pour me redresser. J'ai du mal à marcher, non mais tu te rends compte? Oh mon Dieu, je vous en prie, faites quelque chose pour moi! Aidez cette pauvre femme à retrouver la raison, elle est folle, c'est une folle! Je vous en supplie mon Dieu, aidez-moi à surmonter cette épreuve! Je veux bien souffrir comme le Christ sur la croix mais aidez-moi…[45]

The YOUNGER NUN, her face distraught, kneels down and prays under her breath.

YOUNG:
Lord, forgive me...

The OLDER NUN, crying, lies on the floor flat on her belly and, in stretching out her arms like a cross, this time she does not bump the doll. NICOLA is still on the floor when the two nuns get up and move toward the second chair in the row to expose another patient by lifting the sheet covering his small, curled up body.

Dancers

◆

Lengthy stage directions for the pronoun it

I know that love
Can turn white
As when one sees a dawn
That was believed lost.[46]

— ALDA MERINI
from "La donna di picche"
in *Clinica dell'abbandono*

CHARACTERS:

SHE

HE

*Two open trunks occupy opposite ends of a room. A very old woman is
hunched over the smaller trunk. She searches, she leans over, she loses her
balance, until, struggling, she pulls herself up. She stretches her back and a
wheeze escapes her chest. She holds a switch connected to an electric cable. The
woman presses the switch and a firmament of stars lights up above her head.
Myriads of little bulbs hanging from the ceiling illuminate the room. A man,
equally old, emerges from the other trunk. He looks at her. He smiles. She
bends over again and pulls out an old suit jacket from the bottom of the trunk.
The two start walking toward each other until they meet in the center of the
room. He is tall and skinny. She is tiny and bent over. Out of habit, she stops
at his right. When they are close to each other they resemble the pronoun it.
She helps him put on the jacket. Slowly, he slides one arm and then the other
inside the slightly creased sleeves. it dances. A slow dance. He, with his chin
resting on her head. She, holding on to his jacket. it falls asleep as they dance.
Turn after turn, they begin to snore. They kiss while they snore, mixing the
sounds of the snoring with the sounds of love-making. He touches her. She lets
him touch her. Their grunts become moans then panting. He unbuttons his
jacket, unzips the fly of his pants. it presses up against each other. He taps her
pelvis with small movements of his own. it has an orgasm.*

*She feels like she's suffocating. She has an asthma attack. She fidgets. Taken
by a whole-body tremor, she moves away from him. He extracts a small bottle
from his jacket pocket, takes out a pill, and holds it out to her. She swallows it
voraciously. She then calms down and takes out a white embroidered handkerchief from inside the sleeve of her blouse. She blows her nose and loses her
balance forward. He supports her with one arm. She puts away the handkerchief, then scratches her thigh. He zips up his pants and pulls out a pocket
watch from his jacket.*

*He counts barely moving his lips: 10…9…8…7… He takes a handful of
confetti out of his pocket and merrily throws them in the air…5…4…3… as
midnight tolls, he sets off a small firecracker. She does not react. He pulls out*

269

a party horn and, as soon as he blows into it, it stretches out into a multicolored paper tongue. Again, she doesn't react. He coughs, puts the party horn back in his pocket, and moves away from her. She watches him move away. He moves toward the bigger trunk. He reaches into it with his hand, then his arm, deeper and deeper. He rummages through. He finds two small, colored paper hats. He's amused. He looks at her. She looks at him. He holds one out to her. She turns to scratch her other thigh. He leans over the trunk, puts away the hats, takes out a toy trumpet, stands up, and begins to blow it, clumsily moving around.

His leg cramps. She looks at him. He asks for help with his eyes. She clenches her fist and raps on her leg. He mimics her, trustingly. The cramp melts away. He puts the toy trumpet back in the trunk and takes out a bottle of spumante. She looks at him. He looks at her. it looks at each other for an infinite time. Then she turns toward the opposite side of the room. He puts away the spumante bottle.

She walks toward the smaller trunk. He quickens his step behind her. He follows her. She opens the trunk. She looks inside. She leans over it and, after a few seconds, reappears with a wedding veil on her head. it looks at each other. She has an asthma attack. She feels like she's suffocating. Fidgeting, she gets rid of the veil.

He extracts the bottle out of his pocket, takes out a pill and holds it out to her. She swallows it, then she takes out her handkerchief from inside the sleeve of her blouse and blows her nose, losing her balance forward. He supports her with one arm. She calms down, puts away the handkerchief, then she scratches her thigh.

She bends over again and takes a small music box out of the trunk. it stares at each other. She turns the crank and makes it play. He looks up, sighing. She starts to laugh and move her feet. He laughs too. Laughing and dancing it enters its memories and re-lives backward its love story. She stretches her back, lengthening. He puts on glasses and gets younger. The echo of a song:

> E se domani io non potessi rivedere te... mettiamo il caso tu
> ti sentissi stanco di me... quello che importa all'altra gente non
> mi darà nemmeno l'ombra della perduta felicità... e se domani,

270

*e sottolineo se, all'improvisso perdessi te avrei perduto il mondo
intero non solo te…* [47]

The pronoun it dances.

*Lontano, lontano nel tempo qualche cosa negli occhi di un altro ti
fará ripensare ai miei occhi, i miei occhi che t'amavano tanto… e
lontano, lontano nel mondo…* [48]

it undress: jacket, shirt, skirt, trousers, until he's left in his undershirt and she
in her slip…

*Non essere geloso se con gli altri ballo il twist, non essere geloso se
con gli altri ballo il rock, con te, con te, con te che sei la mia passi-
one, io ballo il ballo del mattone. Lentamente, guancia a guancia,
io ti dico che ti amo, tu mi dici che mi ami, dondolando sulla
stessa mattonella…* [49]

She's thirty-something years-old. He's a few years older.

*Se mi vuoi lasciare dimmi almeno perché… io non so capire per-
ché tu vuoi fuggire… da me… se mi vuoi lasciare dimmi almeno
perché… tu dicevi sempre che vivevi per me… il tuo amore non
era sincero… I tuoi baci non erano veri… I tuoi occhi mi han
sempre mentito…* [50]

Dancing, she moves toward the larger trunk. She lures him swaying her hips.
Aroused, he follows her but as soon as he realizes that a newborn baby has

popped out of the trunk, he runs away as fast as he can. She holds the baby
while she chases him. He runs. She catches up, unloads the baby onto him,
and, still dancing, moves away. He tails her and, as soon as he can, he dumps
his son on her. The baby cries. He regrets what he's done, he goes back, and,
to calm the baby, he starts making strange faces with his mouth, his nose, his
eyes. She also appears to have gone crazy. Both addressing their son, they com-
pete to see who can make the funniest faces and noises.

HE:
An' howcute, howcute, howcute!

SHE:
An' potakatapita!!!

HE and SHE:
An' tuminimipotika!!!

HE:
An' pota...

SHE:
Pota...

HE and SHE:
Potatoe!!

HE:
An' A-Doodle-Doo.

SHE:
An' A-Doodle-Dá.

HE:
Cock-Doodle-A-Doo

SHE:
Cock-Doodle-A-Dá.

HE:
An' papa.

SHE:
An' mama.

HE:
Pppppppupupù.

SHE:
Paepaepaepaepaepaepaè.

HE:
Papapapapapa.

SHE:
An' papa.

HE:
An' papa.

HE and SHE:
An' papa will eat him!

SHE:
You can't eat him!

HIM:
Oh, but I'll eat him! Yes, I'll eat him!

He nibbles the baby.

SHE:

Don't eat him, let him be…leave his tiny hand alone!

HE:

This little hand is mine! I'll eat it! An' the ears are mine as well… I'll eat them… an' the belly button, an' the belly, an' his little pee pee! I'll eat it all, this little pee pee, all of it… all of it…

SHE:

No, not his little pee pee!

HE:

Yes, his little pee pee!

SHE:

Leave his little pee pee alone!

HE:

Yes, yes I'm going to eat it!

SHE:

No!

HE:

Yes!

SHE:

Ahhh!

HE:

An' I'll also eat his little feet! I'm going to eat him all this little baby, all of him!

He bites the new-born baby. He devours him. She tries to take the baby away from him but she can't do it. He tosses the baby in the air and then catches him. Worried, she jumps up with the baby and then falls down. Jumps and falls, jumps and falls until she feels a stabbing pain in her abdomen. She runs toward the other trunk and pulls out a big button-down shirt. She puts it on. She is nine months pregnant. She paces up and down frenetically. She's in labor, about to give birth. He puts the baby in the trunk and follows her, worried.

HE:
Stop and breathe… breathe!

She takes off her shoes. He also takes off his shoes. She hands him her glasses. He puts them in his pocket and then takes his glasses off. She dances from the pain.

Nel continente nero, paraponziponzipò, alle falde del Kilimangiaro, paraponziponzipò… ci sta un popolo di negri che ha inventato tanti balli, il piú famoso è l'Hully-Gully! Hully-Gully, Hully-Gà! [51]

HE:
Breathe, I said!

SHE:
I feel awful!

HE:
Follow me…

SHE:
I'm dying!

HE:

This way, look!

He lifts one leg then the other until he performs the steps to The Watussi dance. She follows his lead, forgetting for a moment that she's in labor...

...Ogni tre passi facciomo sei metri noi siamo quelli che dall'Equatore vediamo per primi le luci del sole... noi siamo i Watussi... [52]

HE:

That's good, sweetie! You see, this way you don't feel the pain anymore!

SHE:

Siamo i Watussi, siaamo i Watussi... gli altissimi negri... ooogni tre passi... ooogni tre passi... [53] Oh! Oh! Oh!

HE:

Facciamo sei metri... [54] Dance and It'll go away!

SHE:

Alle giraffe guardiamo negli occhi, agli elefanti parliamo negli orecchi... se non ci credete venite... venite quaggiù... [55] Ahhh! Ahhh! *Nel continente nero... alle falde del Kilimangiaro... paraponziponzipò...* [56] I'm dying. Run, go get me a sedative... *Paraponziponzipò... paraponziponzipò...* No, no, no... ahhh! Go get me a cigarette... chamomile... make me some chamomile tea... Call... call... call...

HE:

Who should I call?

SHE:

The hospital… my mother… the neighbor… wake up the whole
building… ahhh! Ahhh! *Paraponziponzipò… paraponziponzipò…*
Heeeelpp!

*She takes off the shirt and gives it to him. He puts it on, taking his turn expe-
riencing the excruciating pain. She catches her breath. He takes off the shirt
and looks at her, exhausted. it laughs. He brushes against her breasts. it kisses
and caresses each other. They're aroused. She takes off his undershirt. He, her
slip. She unzips his pants. it gets undressed while dancing.*

> *Dimmi quando tu verrai, dimmi quando quando quando…
> l'anno, il giorno, l'ora in cui forse tu mi bacerai… Ogni instante
> attenderò fino a quando quando quando… d'improvviso ti vedrò
> sorridente accanto a me. Se vuoi dirmi di sì… devi dirlo perché
> non ha senso per me la mia vita senza te… e baciando mi dirai
> non ci lasceremo mai…*[57]

*She moves away from him. He looks at her moving away. She slips inside the
larger trunk. He waits. She comes out wearing a wedding dress.*

> *Ogni instante attenderó fino a quando quando quando… d'im-
> provviso ti vedró sorridente accanto a me…* [58]

*He can't take his eyes off of her but he remains still. He's moved by the sight of
his young bride.*

HE:

Come here! Come!

She holds the music box in her hands. She plays it while she slowly draws close to him, moving like a mechanical doll. it is less than twenty years old. She bends over. She spins around. She moves in spurts. The wedding gown slips off of her. When she stops in front of him, she's wearing a swimming suit. He looks at her in ecstasy. He's also wearing a swimming suit. She hands him the music box. He quickly takes it and hides it behind his back.

HE:
I brought you something.

SHE:
What is it?

HE:
Guess?

She tries to peek behind his back.

Aha aha! Touch my nipple.

As soon as she presses her finger on his nipple, he plays the music box.

The other nipple!

She brushes the other nipple.

Again!

She touches his navel and he plays.

SHE:
But how do you do that?

HE:
Where you touch me, there I make music! Here!

He offers her the music box.

SHE:
What is it?

HE (*mispronouncing the French*):
A *carillon.*

SHE:
You don't pronounce it like that, you dummy!

HE:
Fine, what does it matter?! Do you like it?

SHE:
I like it.

HE:
And I like you.

He's embarrassed. She looks down and plays with the music box. Then she smiles mischievously.

HE:
I like your eyes... I melt when you look at me like that! I like it when
you laugh... like now, you get a dimple here! (*He touches the corner of his
mouth.*) I like your curls, it's like they say: "A whim for every curl!" And I
like when you smoke a cigarette leaning on the balcony hiding from your
father. And I walk back and forth, back and forth under that balcony...

SHE:
I did see you!

HE:
I know... that's why I walk by!

Pause

Do you want to marry me?

*She pulls her head up. Serious, they look at each other. Then, they kiss for the
first time...*

> *...È un'ora che aspetto davanti al portone, su trova una scusa per
> uscire di casa... fatti mandare dall mamma a prendere il latte...
> devo dirti qualcosa che riguarda noi due...*[59]

She breaks away from him and runs wildly, beside herself.

SHE:
Yeees!

*...Ti ho visto uscire dalla scuola insieme ad un altro... con la
mano nella mano passeggiava con te... tu digli a qual coso che
sono geloso che se lo rivedo gli spaccherò il muso... dài scendi
amore... ho bisogno di te... ho bisogno di te... vieni giù...*[60]

Joyfully, he chases her. He catches her, kisses her passionately. She slips away
and rolls on the floor, he follows her. it jumps, summersaults, cartwheels. They
are happy and in love.

*Dài scendi amore... ho bisogno di te... ho bisogno di te... vieni
giù... dài...*[61]

She runs. Her muscles are tensed. Her legs are long and slender. He catches
up with her and hugs her, encircling her with his wide shoulders. it is in love.
She snuggles into his right side and looks toward us. He also looks at us. As if
enchanted, it stares at us.

*...E bà e bè... embè ma che cos'è... kiss me besame t'embrasse
baciami... ba ba baciami piccina sulla bo bo bocca piccolina...
dammi tanti tanti baci in quantità... ma questi baci a chi li devo
dar?... e bì e bò e bù... bi e bè cara sillaba com'è... sono tanto
deliziose queste sillabe d'amore... bi bi bimbo biricchino...*[62]

After she passes him his undershirt and shirt, she puts her blouse back on. it
kisses and starts dancing again while they get dressed. She takes the bottle of
spumante out of the larger trunk and runs toward him. He uncorks it making it
pop.

HE:
Happy New Year!

Questo bacio che cos'è... è un'apostrofo rosa messo nella frase t'amo... ba ba baciami piccina con la bo bo bo bocca piccolina... dammi tanti tanti baci in quantità... ma questi baci a chi li devo dar?...[63]

HE:

Best wishes, my love!

He kisses her again. They drink from the bottle while they continue to get dressed. They laugh. They fall. They get back up. They hug. it gets drunk. He takes the colorful party hats out of the trunk: he puts one on his head and the other on hers. He takes out the toy trumpet and toots it while dancing in an odd but energetic way. She's entertained. He's happy to entertain her.

Laggiù nell'Arizona terra di sogni e di chimere se una chitarra suona cantano mille capinere... hanno la chioma bruna hanno la febbre in cor... chi va a cercar fortuna vi troverà l'amor...[64]

She starts putting away her wedding veil in the smaller trunk, then the music box...

...A mezzanotte va la ronda del piacere e nell'oscurità ognuno vuol godere... son baci di passion... l'amor non sa tacere e questa è la canzon di mille capinere... il bandolero stanco scende la sierra misteriosa sul suo cavallo bianco spicca la vampa di una rosa... quel fior di primavera vuol dire fedeltà e alla sua capinera egli lo porterà...[65]

*He gets more and more drunk. He puts on his trousers, the vest, the bow-tie.
As soon as she puts her jacket on, her back hunches over. He steps inside the
larger trunk and disappears.*

*She puts her wedding dress back inside the smaller trunk together with her
other memories. She's drunk. She bends over the trunk and re-appears with
the face of an old woman. She has an asthma attack. She feels like she's suffocating. Distressed, she looks around and sees his jacket on the floor. She drags
herself toward it. She bends down to pick it up and takes the pill bottle out of
an inside pocket. As she takes out one pill, she spills the others on the floor. She
swallows the pill, takes her handkerchief from inside the sleeve of her blouse,
and blows her nose. She calms down, puts away the handkerchief. She takes
his jacket and brushes off the dust from the collar with the tip of her fingers.
Then, she folds it carefully while moving toward the smaller trunk. She opens
it with difficulty and puts the jacket inside. She looks around. Before perma-
nently shutting the trunk, she bends over and picks up the cable attached to
the switch. She presses the switch and the lights above her head go out. In the
middle of the room, only an empty bottle and a few confetti scattered on the
ground remain. She staggers toward the bottle. She stops and crouches down
breathing heavily.*

*She looks around once more. She's motionless for a few seconds before leaping
with feline agility along the perimeter of the room. Her muscles tighten, her
limbs stretch. She rummages everywhere. Like a caged animal, she sniffs
the air.*

NOTES

Introduction

1. *Mezzogiorno* is a common term to refer to the Southern regions of Italy.
2. Also see Linda Hutcheon, *A Theory of Adaptation* (New York: Routledge, 2006).

mPalermu

3. Translated by Francesca Spedalieri.

4. Grandma Citta speaks in Neapolitan throughout the play, while everyone else speaks in Sicilian unless otherwise noted. She speaks with a different inflection.

5. *Giaculatorias* are short prayers recited from memory in a continuous, often monotonous litany.

6. Translation: "It hurts!"

7. Translation: "Of course we must go out!"

8. Meaning: "Yeah; uh-huh; right."

9. Translation: "A little bit!"

10. Dear little Mimmo. A term of endearment.

11. Luca Toni was lovingly nicknamed Cabubi after the magic flying camel Kaboobie, which appeared in the 1967 American cartoon *Shazzan* that was broadcasted in Italy in the early 1980s by few private TV channels. This nickname was given to Toni because his head-plays were legendary.

12. This is a combination of a noise and a movement meaning "no," a gesture commonly found in Sicily. The noise is a palatoalveolar click, described by the International Phonetic Alphabet (IPA) as a double barred pipe (ǂ). This is a type of click in the non-pulmonic consonants family as described in the Interactive IPA App by Paul Meier. The movement accompanying the sound quickly brings the tongue to the hard palate while the top of the head inclines backward and the chin is brought forward before restoring to a neutral position.

13. In Sicily, water is often rationed due to shortages. During water shortages, "water days" alternate with "non-water days." On water days, a steady water supply reaches citizens' homes, allowing them to stock up on water for use during non-water days. In extreme drought, a water day could occur every three days.

14. Translation: "I'm ready!
    Let's go out.
    Rosalia? Mom's ready! Hurry up!
    Mimmo? Mi?
    Let's go, I'm ready! You hear?
    Giammarco, get Grandma Citta, we'll bring her to the beach."
15. Translation: "should we go out"?

The Butchery

16. Translated by Wayland Young.
17. Metallic street illuminations used during Italian folk and religious festivals.
18. Diminutive: "little Nina." A term of endearment.
19. Translation: "my little darling." Endearing.
20. Lyrics from the song "Amore, amore mio" by Luigi Tenco.
Translation: "My love, my love, my love… I have nothing in this world except a thousand hours to dedicate to you…"
21. Translation: "Look here!"
22. Translation: "Yeah; uh-uh; right."
23. Diminutive: "Little Ignazio." A term of endearment.
24. Translation: "Come on."
25. Diminutive: Toruccio is a form of endearment for Totò, which is a shortened form for Salvatore.
26. Translation: "dressed like a girl."
27. Mispronounciation of "Potemkin."
28. Another line from the song "Amore, amore mio" by Luigi Tenco
Translation: "Love, my love, these empty hands of mine are full of caresses only for you…"

Life of Mine

29. Translation: "Yes."
30. Toni Goal is the nickname of the soccer player Luca Toni. Toni led the Palermo soccer team to the Serie A (the Italian First Division League) scoring twenty goals in one season.

Market Dogs

31. Translated by Francesca Spedalieri.
32. A city that is both mother and matrix.

33. Meaning: "Yeah; uh-huh; right."
34. Translation: "I MOTHER DELIVER ITALY TO YOU."

Holywater

35. Translated by Francesca Spedalieri.
36. Translation: "Holywater."
37. A Neapolitan word that describes a feeling of lethargic, apathetic helplessness and longing.
38. 'O Granatiello or, in Italian, Il Granatello, is an area in the town of Portici.
39. Lyrics from the Neapolitan song "Maruzzella" by Renato Carosone. Translation: "Oh! Who hears and who now sings after me… Oh, even the moon peaks out to see, overlooking the whole marina from Procida to Resina, it asks look there, what's that woman doing?… Dear little Marisa, you've put the sea in your eyes and you've put sadness in my heart… this heart you make beat stronger than the waves when the sky's dark… first you say yes, then you sweetly let me die… Dear little Marisa…"
40. Idem.
41. Lyrics from the song "Indifferentemente" by Mario Abbate. Translation: "The moon sets… and we, to play the last scene, are left hand in hand, without having the courage to look at each other… Do of me what you will… indifferently, because I know what I am: for you now I'm nothing! Just give me this poison, don't wait till tomorrow… indifferently… if you kill me, I'm not going to say anything."

The Zisa Castle

42. Translated by Stanisław Barańczak and Clare Cavanagh.
43. Translation: "Stop it! Stop it! I beg you! For the love of God, stop it! You're hurting me, really hurting! I can't go on like this, I, I can't take it anymore! I've reached the end, the limit of what's bearable! I've got enormous bruises on my behind, bruises this big! I put on ointment every night before going to bed but it doesn't do anything! My rear end is all swollen. I suffer, I! Do you realize what you've made me suffer for years? I can't go on like this, no, it's not possible! In the morning, when I get up, I feel so terrible I double over, like this! I have to put in a superhuman effort just to pull myself up. I struggle to walk, no but you do realize it, don't you? Oh God, please, do something for me! Help this poor woman see reason, she's crazy, she's a madwoman! I beseech you, my Lord, help me overcome this trial! I'm willing to suffer like Christ on the cross but help me…"
44. Meaning: "Yeah; uh-huh; right."
45. See note 43 for translation.

Dancers

46. Translated by Francesca Spedalieri.

47. Lyrics from the song "E se domani." Music by Carlo Alberto Rossi. Lyrics by Giorgio Calabrese.
Translation: "And if tomorrow I couldn't see you again… let's say you'd grown tired of me… what's important to other people would not give me even the shadow of my lost happiness… and if tomorrow, and I stress if, I were to suddenly lose you I would have lost the whole world and not only you…"

48. Lyrics from the song "Lontano lontano." Music and Lyrics by Luigi Tenco.
Translation: "faraway, faraway in time something in somebody's eyes will make you think of my eyes, my eyes that loved you so… and faraway, faraway in the world…"

49. Lyrics from the song "Il ballo del mattone." Music by Dino Verde. Lyrics by Bruno Canfora.
Translation: "Don't be jealous if with others I dance the twist, don't be jealous if with others I dance the rock, with you, with you who are my passion, I dance the brick dance. Slowly, cheek to cheek, I tell you that I love you, you tell me that you love me, swaying on the same tile…"

50. Lyrics from the song "Se mi vuoi lasciare." Music by Gian Piero Reverberi. Lyrics by Saro Leva.
Translation: "If you want to leave me, at least tell me why… I don't understand why you'd want to flee… from me… if you want to leave me, at least tell me why… you always said you lived for me… your love wasn't sincere… your kisses weren't true… your eyes have always lied to me…"

51. Lyrics from the song "I Watussi." Music by Edoardo Vianello. Lyrics by Carlo Rossi.
Translation: "In the dark continent, paraponziponzipò, at feet of the Kilimanjaro, paraponziponzipò… there's a country of black people who have invented many dances, the most famous is the Hully-Gully! Hully-Gully, Hully-Gá!"

52. Ibid.
Translation: "…every three steps we do six meters, we are the ones that from the Equator first glimpse at the light of the sun… we are the Watussi…"

53. Ibid.
Translation: "We are the Watussi, we aare the Watussi… the tallest black people… eeevery three steps… eeevery three steps…"

54. Ibid.
Translation: "We do six meters."

55. Ibid.
Translation: "We look giraffes in the eyes, we speak into elephants' ears… if you don't believe it come… come down here."

56. Ibid.

Translation: "In the dark continent... at the feet of the Kilimanjaro, paraponzi-ponz-ipó..."

57. Lyrics from the song "Quando, Quando, Quando (Tell Me When)." Music by Tony Renis. Original Italian Lyrics by Alberto Testa.

Translation: "Tell me when you'll come, tell me when when when... the year, the day, the hour when, maybe, you'll kiss me... Each instant I'll wait until when when when... suddenly I'll see you smiling next to me. If you want to tell me yes... you'll have to say it because my life doesn't make sense without you... and kissing me you'll tell me that we'll never leave each other..."

58. Ibid.

Translation: "Each instant I'll wait until when when when... suddenly I'll see you smiling next to me..."

59. Lyrics from the song "Fatti mandare dalla mamma." Music by Luis Enriquez Bacalov. Lyrics by Franco Migliacci.

Translation: "It's an hour I'm waiting in front of your door, come on find an excuse to get out of the house... have your mother send you to get some milk... I have to tell you something that's about us..."

60. Ibid.

Translation: "...I saw you getting out of school with another guy... hand in hand he was walking with you... tell that thing that I'm jealous and that if I see him again, I'll smash his face... come on come down love... I need you... I need you... come down..."

61. Ibid.

Translation: "come on, come down love... I need you... I need you... come down... come on..."

62. Lyrics from the song "Ba ba baciami piccina." Music by Luigi Astore. Lyrics by Riccardo Morbelli.

Translation: "An' ki an' kae... so what's this here?... baciami besame t'embrasse kiss me... ki ki kiss me darling baby on the ma ma mouth darling baby... give me give me many kisses give me plenty... but these kisses who should I give them to?... an' ka an' ko an' ku... ka an' kae dear syllable, how is it?... they're so delicious these syllables of love... nau nau naughty little child..."

63. Ibid.

Translation: "This kiss, what is it?... It's the rosy apostrophe in the line "lovin' you"... ki ki kiss me darling baby on the ma ma mouth little one... give me give me many kisses give me plenty... but these kisses who should I give them to?..."

64. Lyrics from the song "Il tango delle capinere." Music by Cesare Andrea Bixio. Lyrics by Bixio Cherubini.

Translation: "Down there in Arizona, land of dreams and chimeras, if a guitar plays

a thousand blackcap birds sing… they have dark manes and a fever in their heart…
who goes looking for fortune there will find love…"

65. Ibid.

Translation: "At midnight the pleasure rounds begin, and in the darkness everyone
wants to be pleased… they're kisses of passion… love doesn't know how to be quiet
and this is the song of a thousand blackcap birds… the tired bandolero comes down
from the mysterious sierra, on his white horse the striking flame of a rose… that
spring flower means fidelity and he'll bring it to his blackcap bird…"

Swan Isle Press is a not-for-profit publisher
of poetry, fiction, and nonfiction.

For information on books of related interest or
for a catalog of new publications contact:
www.swanislepress.com

mPalermo, Dancers, and Other Plays
Designed by Marianne Jankowski
Typeset in Adobe JensonPro
Printed on 55# Natural Offset Antique